ZERO TO DATA VIZ

as a Tableau Desktop Specialist

John Zugelder, CFA

Zero to Data Viz as a Tableau Desktop Specialist

By John Zugelder

Published by JZ Analytics Press 2020, Garland, TX

www.tableaudesktopspecialist.com

Cover design: Jak Krumholtz

ISBN: 978-0-578-75424-6

Introduction

The future of employment hinges on people's ability to understand and interact with technology and algorithms. The proliferation of artificial intelligence (AI) and Machine Learning, means much of the future will be automated. Those of us with the skills to understand data and automation will have work for decades to come, but the real job security and value multiplier is the ability to tie the thread between the data and human elements.

Visuals were an essential part of human communication before we had language. We used cave drawings and stone carvings in the beginning, and the earliest maps date back to the BC epoch. These hand-drawn visual displays of information evolved with time and technological advances, such as paper, the printing press, and ultimately computers.

In the current, digital age, computers managed to abstract most elements of life into 1s and 0s for representation in computer software, data, and visuals. The current explosion of information means that we create data about almost everything, and we have more data than we can manage.

In a business context, using all this information is essential for driving positive outcomes that improve the lives of the people and communities our businesses serve. As individuals, this creates an incredible opportunity to expand our skills, and get back tot he human element of storytelling.

Data visualization is all about storytelling with thoughtfully crafted images that layer information and insights.

With the human eye's ability to process 10Mb/s of visual data, a well-designed graphic delivers instant insight through layers of visual information in a single image. Learning to create powerful, layered visuals empowers us to deliver these insights that help combine the power of automation through AI and Machine learning with the human skills required to truly improve society's material well-being. This collaborative intersection between humans and technology is the future of work and life.

There are many tools available for building data visualizations, but the consistent leader in this space is Tableau. Tableau offers connectors to the widest variety of data sources, powerful analysis capability, extensive customization, and its feature list continues to expand.

This book mixes practical Tableau techniques and data visualization theory and best practice to prepare you for the Tableau Desktop Specialist certification exam, and it will arm you with the essential tools to build your Tableau Public portfolio. With your portfolio and certification, there will be no shortage of opportunities professionally and charitably to make an impact through visual storytelling.

These are the 2 most important pieces of information you need to start your Tableau journey:

1. **Be Curious.** Data analysis and visualization is all about exploring data for answers to real-world questions, and learning Tableau is all about exploring what happens when you click, drag, and drop.

2. **Undo.** The keyboard shortcut, "Ctrl + Z" (Windows) or "Command + Z" (Mac), and the back arrow in the Tableau toolbar will undo your changes. This makes it hard to break things. You can always undo the last few actions so don't be afraid to investigate what happens when you click around.

    *   The forward arrow in the toolbar will redo the action, and it's keyboard shortcut is "Ctrl + Y" (Windows) or "Command + Shift + Z" (Mac),

Many of you could stop there and figure out everything you need to know to pass the exam, but if you continue reading, I'll help you get there faster.

About Me

As you may have seen on the back cover, I am an economist / statistician, who likes to play with data. I've worked at a few of the largest banks in the world, analyzing incredible volumes of data. More recently, I've been exploring the world of data for good, and trying to find ways to use public data to produce meaningful insights for the broader benefit of society.

I've always had an interest in random facts, and some of the random facts I learned as a child, are no longer facts. For example, I read in a book once that goldfish have a memory of 3 seconds. When I was in primary school that was a true fact, but scientists have since proven the memory of a goldfish extends up to 5 months! Some facts are still true, and still spark my curiosity. For example, the US President Abraham Lincoln had a secretary named Kennedy, and US President John F. Kennedy had a secretary named Lincoln. Is this a coincidence or something else?

My interest in random facts combined with a love for logic puzzles, and computers, economics, and statistics were a natural fit. In retrospect, I was destined for data science, and along the way, I earned a degree in Economics & Finance degree, a CFA Charter, and a data scientist certificate.

One of my early high school jobs was data entry and beta testing in the healthcare space, and it was an opportunity for me to see data and technology impact positive outcomes in people's lives. Then, when I finished university, my banking and finance career began in a bank branch as a personal banker, opening accounts and running a teller drawer. These early experiences solidified my commitment to helping people, and many of my career highlights are the opportunities to teach and mentor others.

A couple years ago, I started helping a small group of people build their data skills to enhance their employment opportunities in my spare time. While pulling together teaching materials for the this group of aspiring data professionals, a few of them requested printed copy, and I realized that I had enough material for a book.

In addition to writing this book, I teach training courses, and offer one on one coaching.

About the Exam

The Tableau Desktop Specialist Exam was introduced in 2018. As of this writing, the Tableau Desktop Specialist Certification does not expire, while the other more advanced certifications Tableau offers, when they update the test. Test updates generally coincide with major releases of the Tableau software.

The specialist exam is squarely targeted at the basics, offering aspiring data visualization professionals an opportunity to demonstrate a fundamental capability with Tableau.

The exam can be taken in person at the Tableau Conference, or online through remote proctoring service. The online exam requires you to connect to a virtual machine that contains the necessary data and Tableau Desktop software.

The exam has a time limit of 60 minutes, and there will be at least 30 minutes of setup and ID verification. There are 30 questions in total. Approximately 22 questions are multiple choice or multiple response, with the remaining 8 being hands-on.

The questions are weighted based on difficulty so the number of correct questions to pass will vary, and the minimum passing score is 70%. Aiming for 25 correct questions will ensure you pass.

Unlike some of the more advanced Tableau certification exams, there are no constraints to how you answer the hands-on questions. These questions focus on whether you can produce the correct number and/or answer. You have full control over whether you produce a table, bar chart, line graph, or other visualization.

As a guide, the breakdown of exam questions is approximately:

- 8 questions on "Connecting To & Preparing Data"

- 12 questions on "Exploring & Analyzing Data"

- 6 questions on "Understanding Tableau Concepts"

- 4 questions on "Sharing Insights"

Additional information about the exam and computer requirements is available on the Tableau website[1]. A critical piece of information on the site is the version of Tableau desktop used when taking the exam.

About This Book

This book will prepare you for the Tableau Desktop Specialist exam, and it is designed for you to do the majority of your preparation using Tableau Public. The actual test is taken using Tableau Desktop Professional. However, most functionality is identical, and you can leverage the 14 day free trial to familiarize yourself with the small differences between the Desktop and Public versions. I recommend waiting to do this until just before you take the test.

The primary differences between the two versions are live connections, options to save data sources, export options, and the ability to save workbooks to your local machine. I will cover this in more detail in the next section and throughout the book. Additionally, with the student and full Tableau Desktop license you are able to download the exact version of Tableau you will use to take the exam. Currently, Tableau Public is 2020.2 and the exam uses the 2020.1 version. (I will outline the major difference a bit later.)

In the following pages, I endeavor to provide the relevant context and "why" for many of the topics in the book, and this should give you the relevant information to answer the exam questions. After you have a high-level understanding of these core concepts, working with data in Tableau and taking practice quizzes embeds the knowledge and develops the necessary speed for the timed exam.

The book is laid out in the following order:

1. Introduction

2. Connecting to & Preparing Data

3. Understanding Tableau Concepts

4. Exploring and analyzing data

5. Sharing Insights

The sequencing arms you with the foundational grasp of Tableau's mechanics and processing, before moving on to the practical steps of creating the visualizations.

I intentionally kept most topics as brief as possible to provide, with the aim to include only essential information for the exam. However, there are some topics that require additional context for those of us starting from scratch. Also, where feasible, I numbered the images for you to follow along, recreating the visuals presented in the book yourself.

Should you wish to go deeper, I include links to more detailed and advanced information from the Tableau website throughout the book.

The *Zero to Data Viz* companion website[2] contains links to the data used throughout the book, as well as additional resources. As you work through the book, I strongly recommend having Tableau open to recreate the examples yourself.

For improved learning outcomes, finish making your visuals, and compare them to the originals. My Tableau Public profile[3] contains the original workbooks. Use them to check your work.

Also, I want to credit Tableau for the great sample data they created to learn their amazing product. Most of the data used in the examples is widely available online, or as part of the Tableau Desktop installation.

Now, let's install Tableau, and start your data visualization journey!

Installing Tableau Desktop

You can skip this session if you intend to use Tableau Public. However, I recommend revisiting it to do some practice with your 14 day free trial before taking the exam. If you are affiliated with an accredited academic institution, you may be eligible for a free 1 year student license of Tableau. If qualify for the academic access, proceed with downloading the student software, Otherwise, skip this section and come back to it two-weeks before your exam.

To install the current version of Tableau Desktop, go to the Tableau website, and navigate to the Tableau desktop page.

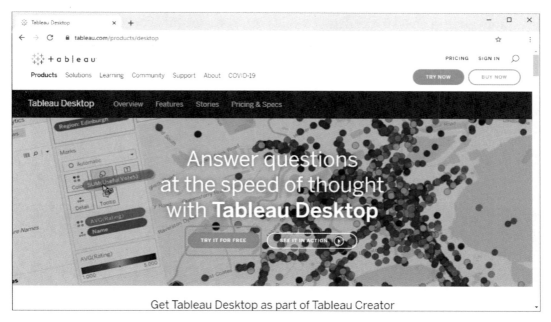

Download Tableau Desktop

Once there, click the try it for free button, and the following page loads.

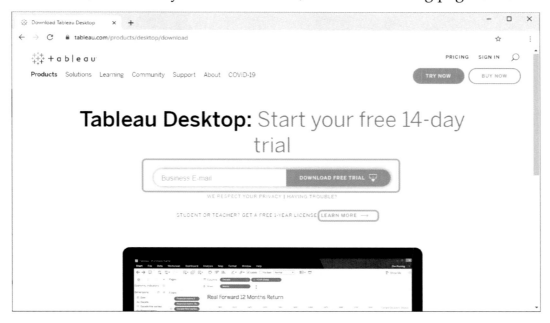

Download installation file

If you qualify for the 1 year student license, click the learn more link. Then, fill out the web form, and download the software.

If you are using the 14 day free trial, enter your email, and click download free trial. Once the download completes, run the installation file, and follow the prompts.

Additionally, you can navigate to the support page to download a prior version of Tableau, if you want the exact version used in the test.

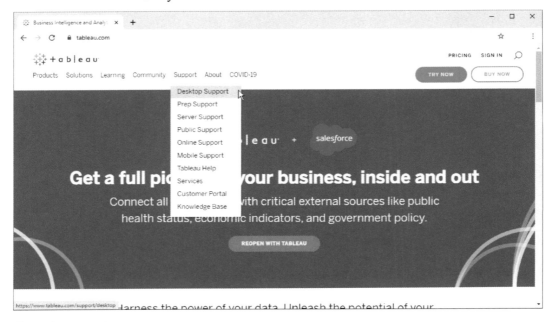

Go to the support page

Clicking "Desktop Support" from the support drop-down menu takes you to the following page.

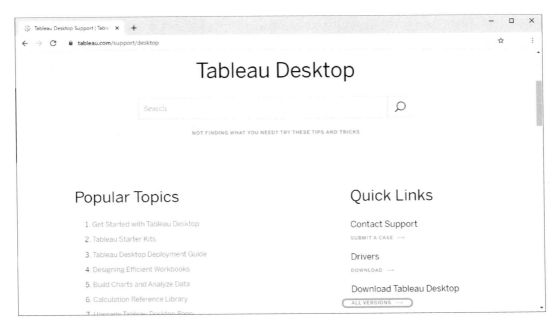

Support Page

Scroll down the page and click the "All Versions" link to load a list of the previous versions of Tableau available for download.

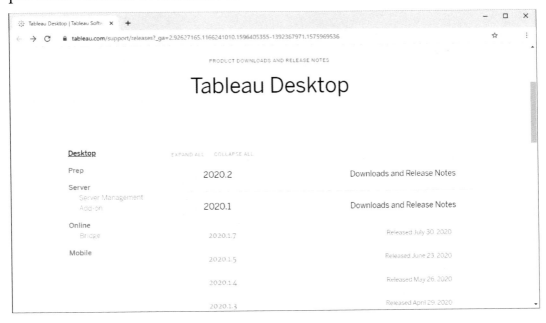

Prior Versions

Click through to the desired version, and it will load a page that contains a download button. Download and run the installation file. The Tableau installation is a standard Windows installation process, and you don't need to change any of the default settings.

Now that you have at least one version of Tableau installed, proceed to the next section. The comparison between Tableau Public and Desktop will help you orient yourself to the Tableau application.

Installing Tableau Public

Tableau Public is available from the Tableau Public website[4], and installation is simple and free. Simply go to the website, enter your email address, and click the download button. The email address you use should be the same email address you will use to setup your Tableau Public Profile.

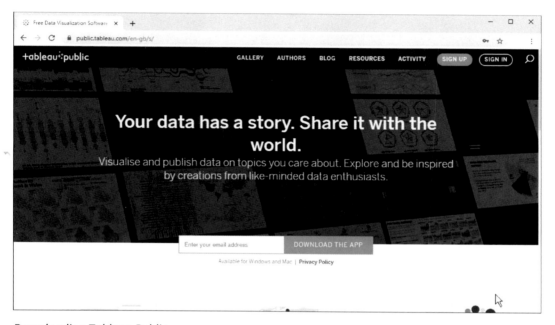

Downloading Tableau Public

After you hit the download button you will come to the following page. Here you have a couple steps to install the application and setup your profile.

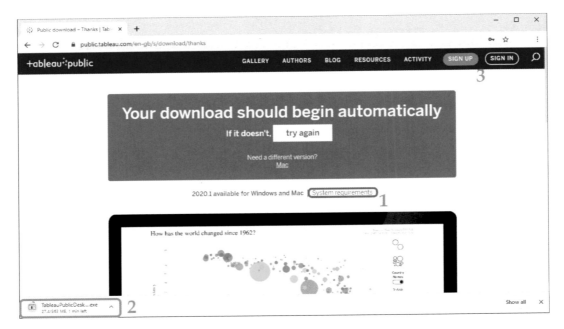

Launch Installer

1. While the file downloads, check the system requirements to confirm your computer has the disk space, processor, memory, and operating system to run Tableau. (Windows: hit the window key and start typing "System" to launch system information. Mac: Click the Apple logo in the top left corner of the desktop, and select "About This Mac")

2. Click the file to launch the installer once the download is complete. This is a standard Windows installation process, and you shouldn't need to change the default settings.

3. Sign-up for your Tableau Public account so that you can save workbooks to your Tableau Public profile. This is the only way to save your work in Tableau Public.

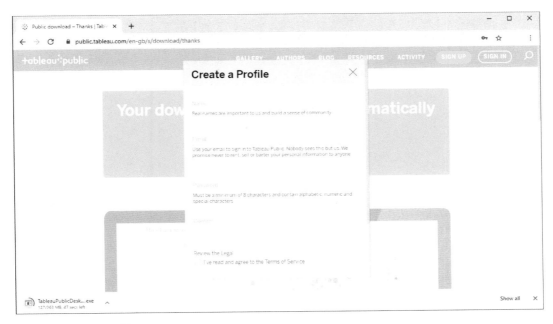

Create Tableau Profile

For now, your Tableau Public profile is your learning space, so don't worry about the content. After you pass the Tableau Desktop Specialist exam, you can curate the content into a portfolio of work. The specialist certification helps you land an interview, and being able to talk through your portfolio helps you land the job.

Additionally, your Tableau Public profile helps integrate you into a supportive community of Tableau users, and you'll be able to save your work using the free Tableau Public software.

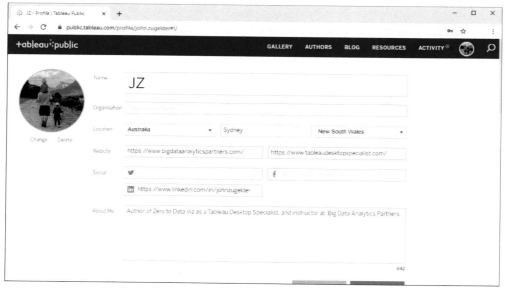

Tableau Profile Detail

Now that you've installed Tableau Public and setup your profile, let's open Tableau for the first time. Navigate to Tableau in your Start menu (Windows), the Applications launchpad on Mac, or the desktop icon if you created one, and start Tableau Public. When Tableau opens, it will bring you to the Tableau Start Page. The image below labels the different elements of the Tableau Start Page.

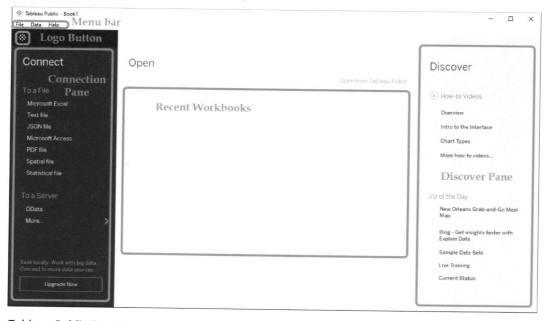

Tableau Public Start Page

- The menu bar contains drop-down menus for the available actions depending on your location in Tableau.

    - File is where you create, save, and open workbooks, and there is also an option to edit your Tableau Public Profile, which opens your web browser.

    - Data has an option for pasting data from your clipboard into Tableau, and eventually includes actions related to any connected data.

    - Help includes settings and links to additional resources

- The logo button toggles between the initial connection screen and the most recently active workbook sheet

- The connection pane includes the available options for connecting to data files and servers

- The recent workbooks section will include thumbnails of recent workbooks.

- The "Open from Tableau Public" link in orange brings up a login prompt for you to connect to your Tableau Public profile, and then you can open any of the workbooks saved to your profile.

- The discover pane includes links to Tableau's online learning resources, as well as links to recent visualizations they've highlighted as the "Viz of the Day." These are a great source of inspiration and ideas.

There is a slight difference to the Tableau Start Page when using the fully licensed Tableau Desktop software. The Tableau Desktop screen, includes icons at the bottom for Sample Workbooks, and it includes a link to additional samples. The connection pane includes a wider range of options for connecting to data sources, along with a section on saved data sources (More on those later). There is also a server option that appears in the menu bar, and finally, it includes slightly different resources and links in the discover pane.

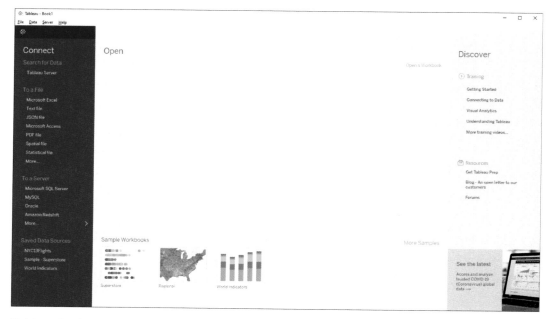

Tableau Desktop Start Page

There are additional differences between Tableau Public and the paid license Tableau Desktop software, with respect to connection types, saved data sources, exporting images, and saving / opening Tableau workbooks. We will discuss these differences throughout the book, but they do not make a material difference with respect to preparing for the Tableau Desktop Specialist Exam. Once you've covered the material in this book, you can download a free trial of the full Tableau Desktop to do your final exam prep. The test will be taken on a virtual environment running Tableau Desktop.

Open a Workbook from Tableau Public

Tableau Desktop saves the details on the data source and visualizations in a Tableau workbook file format to your local hard drive, Tableau Server, or Tableau Public.

Tableau Public is only able to save and open workbooks from Tableau Public. All the visualization capability is there, but Tableau Public lacks the ability to save workbook files.

Opening a workbook from Tableau Public is straight forward. Navigate to Tableau Public in your web browser and click the download button from a user's profile or within the viz directly.

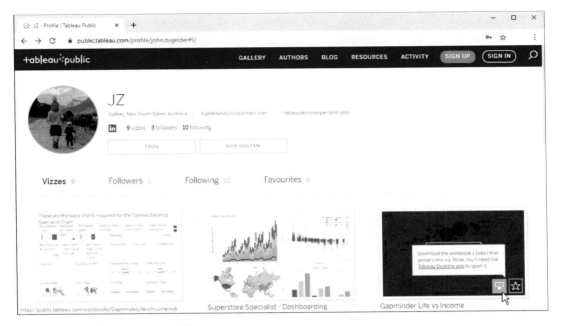

Download workbook from profile

The download button is available when hovering over the visualization's thumbnail in a user profile.

It also appears when you open the visualization in your browser. These buttons immediately download the workbook file.

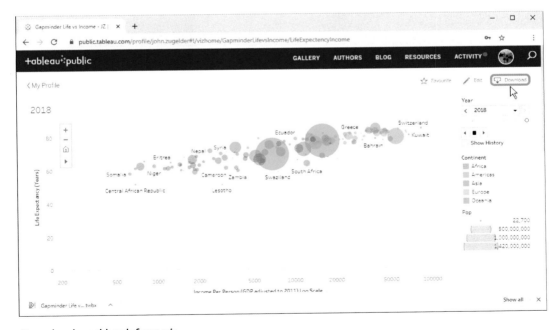

Download workbook from viz

Alternatively, there is a download button in the bottom of the Tableau Public visualization, providing a few format options for download.

Download formats from viz

1. Click the download button.

2. Select your desired format in the pop-up menu.

Now, open the workbook, and you're ready to go.

Elements of the worksheet

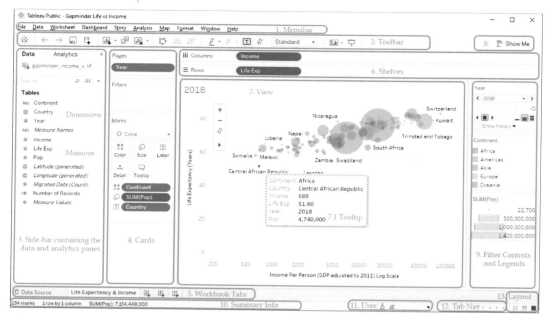

The Tableau Workspace

Here are the core elements of the worksheet window:

1. Menubar- The menubar consists of the drop-down menus that contain the options or settings for different elements of the Tableau workbook.

    - File lists options for opening, closing, and saving the workbook. (In the full desktop version, it also contains print and export options.)

    - Data, Worksheet, Dashboard, and Story list the options and settings for those respective tabs in the workbook.

    - Analysis, Map, and Format list the options and settings for their respective components of the current sheet. (There are also a few workbook level settings.)

    - Window contains a couple of display options, as well as a full list of the tabs in the workbook that can be used for navigation.

2. Toolbar - The toolbar includes buttons for some of the frequently used items in the menus from the menu bar

3. Side-Bar - The side bar contains the data and analytics panes.

- The data pane contains the available data sources in the workbook and their respective dimensions and measures.

- The analytics pane contains tools for performing advanced analytical tasks.

4. Cards - Cards proved specific controls / customization of the worksheets, and they can appear on either side of the view.

   - Pages allows the visualization to be split across separate discrete pages, for example, by year in the Gapminder graphic above. This creates a play functionality, where Tableau progresses through each page like a slideshow, or flip book.

   - Filters controls the filters applied to the worksheet.

   - Marks control customization for the visual, including color, size, text, detail, and tool tip.

5. Workbook Tabs - The sheet tabs navigate to the data source page, existing visualization worksheets, and can create a new worksheet, dashboard, or story tan within the workbook.

6. Shelves - The shelves allocate the data fields used to either columns or rows in the view.

7. View - The view contains the current visualization, and is the primary work space for adjusting axes and other options.

   - Tooltip - Hovering over a mark in the view produces a customizable tooltip with additional detail. Clicking the mark adds various buttons depending on the mark.

8. Show Me Button - Toggles the "Show Me" menu, which displays the charts Tableau can automatically generate based on the selected dimensions and measures in the data pane.

9. Legends & Filter Controls - Tableau places legends and filter controls in this section by default, but you can drag them around the window.

10. Summary Info - At the bottom of left, in the status bar, Tableau will display summary metrics based on the view and selection.

11. Current User - Here you can see the current user and log out.

12. Navigation - These arrows navigate through the different tabs in the workbook.

13. Layout buttons - The buttons toggle between different ways to view the tabs in the worksheet.

For more detailed explanations of the work space and view space, check out the Tableau website's reference page[5].

Interact with a Viz

Tableau is an incredible tool for an analyst to tell a story, but the real power is the chart interaction for the viewer. A well crafted visual piques the viewer's curiosity, and then, it contains the interactive elements for the viewer to answer their questions. Let's explore the Gapminder visualization.

What was the life expectancy in Switzerland in 2018? (Try hovering over Switzerland to see the answer.)

Is this the country with the highest life expectancy?

Now, take a minute with the Gapminder visual to explore how Tableau shifts and changes based on your page selection of year in the top right of the filters and controls sections. What was life expectancy in 1820?

What happens when you click on the forward or backward arrow in the page control?

How does the playback change when you select a continent in the color legend?

Take a few minutes to continue exploring the view. Then, try to create a new sheet a new sheet, and see what happens when you just start clicking, double clicking, and dragging fields from the data pain into the different cards and parts of the view.

Armed with a high level overview of data visualization and the Tableau software, you're ready to learn the theory and concepts covered on the Tableau Desktop Specialist exam. First up, is connecting to and preparing data.

Connecting to & Preparing Data

Learning Outcome

Once we connect Tableau to the data, it is easy to start creating visuals. Understanding Tableau's data mechanics frees up mental capacity for design and interpretation of data.

By the end of this section you will understand:

- why tableau prefers long data to wider, cross-tab data

- the various methods and data sources Tableau uses to connect to data

- when to trade the performance of extracts for the recency of live data

- the different ways to link data together using joins, unions, and blends

- how to manage data properties such as field names, aliased values, data types, and default properties

Understanding this foundational knowledge expedites the visualization development and refinement process, as you as you progress through the design and creations of visualizations, dashboards, and stories.

What is Data?

Data is information stored for retrieval and use by humans and/or computers. There are many formats for storing data, such as documents, spreadsheets, flat files (text), and databases. Out of the current suite of available data visualization tools, Tableau has one of the most comprehensive libraries in terms of connectors. Without getting too technical, connectors are code libraries so that Tableau can read and manipulate data from a variety of sources and file types.

In addition to formats, it is important to consider the layout of the data when connecting to Tableau. Tableau does well with long tables, which are nicely described by Hadley Wickham as tidy tables. You can read more about it in his paper from the Journal of Statistical Software[6].

The condensed summary is that the more granular the dataset the more calculations and aggregation is possible. Tableau can create a much larger array of visual analytics with tables containing a row for each record or observation. As an example, here are two different layouts of rainfall measurements from the Australian Bureau of Meteorology website. The data includes daily rainfall measurements from the Sydney Botanic Gardens' station. This first layout is a crosstab format, with multiple observations per row.

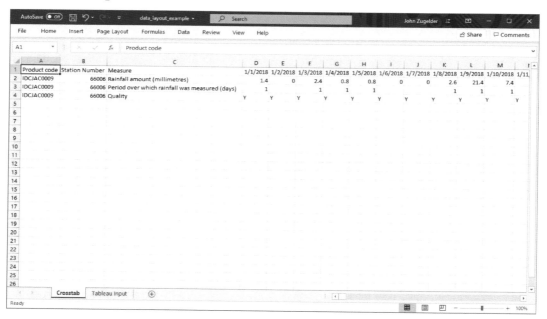

Crosstab data format

While Tableau can connect and use this format, the format drastically hinders the full power of Tableau's analytical capability. To get the most out of Tableau, the data should look like this.

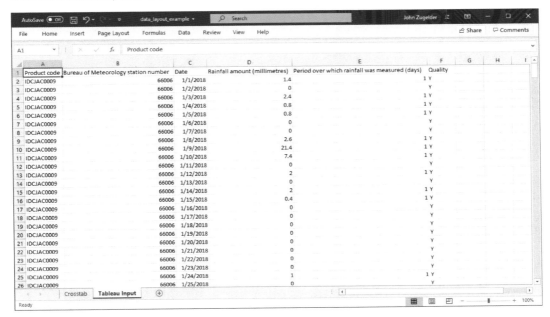

Long table

This second layout contains two rainfall measure columns, with only one observation per row. If you need to see a crosstab view, Tableau can quickly produce one, and since the data is in a long, or tidy, format Tableau can also do so much more. Let's start in on connecting to the data so we can get to that "so much more" part!

Create and modify data connections

Tableau can connect to and use almost all types of data, and the Tableau community is creating new custom data connectors all the time. A full list of data connectors is available here on the Tableau site[7].

When first opened, Tableau displays a *connection pane* on the left side of the start screen. The connection pane is where you select which type of data you plan to use. Notice the top section is "To a File", and the second section is "To a Server."

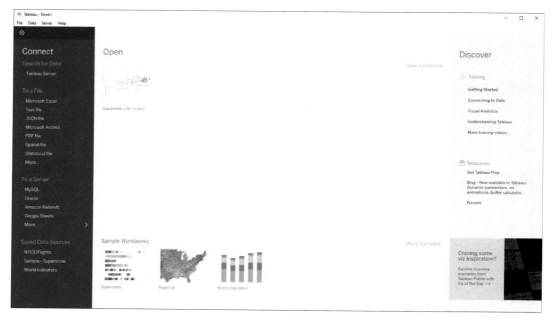

Tableau Desktop Connection Pane

Pictured above, the bottom of the connection pane contains the saved connections, when using Tableau Desktop.

The image below is the same screen from Tableau Public, where the "Upgrade Now" button replaces the saved data connections.

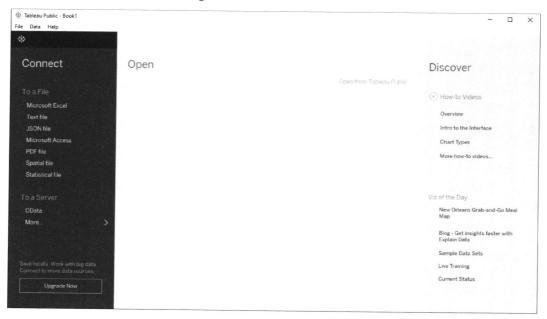

Tableau Public Connection Pane

Connecting to data

When you connect to a data server, the data pane will display a list of schema, and tables for you to add. When you connect to a spreadsheet file, Tableau will list out the sheets contained in the file. When using a text file, Tableau will show all the text files in the same folder.

As an example, we will use the now ubiquitous Global Superstore data that is included with the Tableau desktop installation, and used in many of their online help videos. The zip file from the *Zero to Data Viz* companion site contains an Excel workbook with an orders sheet and a people sheet, in addition to a ".csv" file with returns data. The data covers a few years worth of sales for a global office supplies store.

First, connect Tableau to the Excel spreadsheet, by using the connection pane or dragging the file from the folder into the Tableau window. Tableau lists all of the sheets in the workbook, and once you drag the orders sheet into the data space, Tableau generates a preview of the data. Dragging additional sheets into the data space begins linking the data together. This can be done with joins, unions, blends, and the newer relationships feature.

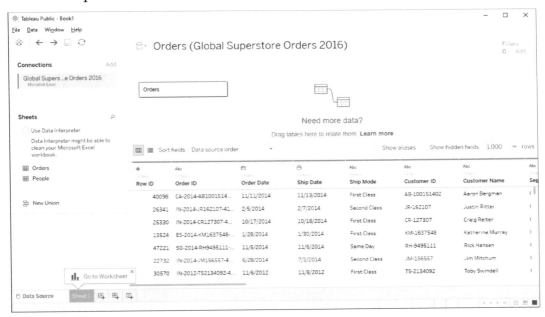

Connect to data 2020.2 and newer

By default, Tableau 2020.2, and newer versions, use relationships. The data canvas is slightly modified from prior versions, as pictured above. Previously the data sources tab displayed all fields from the joined or unioned table. Now, the data preview only shows the fields for the selected table in the relationship view.

When using legacy workbooks, created using older versions of Tableau, the data canvas will list a single table named, "Migrated Data," and double-clicking it displays the underlying data tables in the join view.

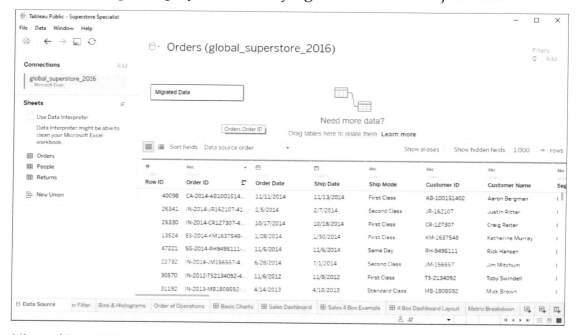

Migrated Data 2020.2 and newer

To access the joins and unions editor, double-click any data table in the canvas, and you can add or edit joins and unions. With the new relationships you may still want to specify a join or a union, when joining on calculations, working with data models unsupported by relationships, or for other reasons.

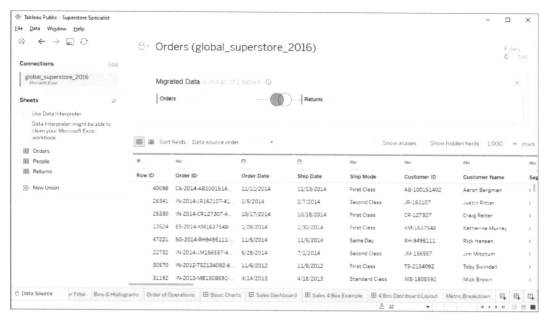

Join Editor 2020.2 and newer

Here is a high-level summary of joins, blends and relationships, before we get into the detail.

Joins	Blends	Relationships
Outputs a single table for use as the Tableau data source	Uses a left join within the worksheet context	Uses logical tables an a deferred join
Use joins add columns of data from consistent row structures	Legacy method for combining data from different levels of detail	Use to combine data from different levels of detail
No context	Always uses worksheet context	Context derived from dimensions used in the table
Physical Layer	Physical Layer	Logical Layer

Relationships

Tableau recently introduced the new concept of relationships, which are context aware connections between data. Traditionally, analysts use programming languages and business intelligence tools to join, union, or blend data from different data tables and sources.

Starting with version 2020.2, Tableau will work out the related fields across tables, and determine the appropriate relationships, automatically. If the field names are not consistent data types and names, you may need to identify the linked fields manually, but Tableau will do the rest.

Relationships work with single tables, star, and snowflake schema. When multiple tables contain measures, Tableau aggregates the measures before joining the data to avoid unnecessary duplication of data.

Using traditional join methods, the join process starts by linking to tables by their key fields or record ids. Then, the data analysis tool aggregates the combined dataset. For example, if we have two tables, one with taxes paid and one with income earned, the traditional join process links the tax id in each table to produce a new, single table (physical) with a column for each field tax id, taxes paid, and income earned.

Data analysis tools aggregate the information from the combined data table. When the same identifier value is present multiple times in an input table, the join produces a record for each occurrence of the id field. This may result in duplication and double counting of values. In the tax example if a person has two incomes from working multiple jobs, the join may inadvertently double count their taxes paid.

The single tax paid for the two incomes will match the tax id for each income record. Using a relationship, Tableau aggregates the total taxes paid by tax id separately from the income earned, and then it links the two values together in a logical layer.

With joins, physical tables are created with all the individual records from the datasets. Tableau matches the keys at a row level, and then creates the new table. When a dataset has two records for the same key field, traditional joins result in a table including both records.

To see how this plays out with actual data, experiment with the orders and returns tables in the Global Superstore dataset to get a feel for how the data works as a relationship, inner join, and other join types. Use the relationship to link the orders and returns. Then read through the joins section and see the difference with the various join options.

With relationships, Tableau aggregates the data from each table before combining the information in the final output. This creates what is known as a logical layer. At the top level, Tableau knows logically that the tables relate on matching fields, but processing is faster the fewer records analysed. By aggregating each table individually, Tableau creates two smaller tables to link, and the aggregation to avoids duplication when there are one to many relationships.

As part of this new approach to data, Tableau replaced it's Number of Records with a field TableName(Count). This makes it easy to pull in the number of records from each table without any calculation logic.

Assumptions & Requirements with Relationships

- The relationship between related fields must be "equal to"

- Related fields need to be the same data type

- There is no capability to define relationships based on geographic fields or calculated fields

- Published data sources are NOT editable and you are NOT able relationships between published data sources

- Relationships are not able to link multiple shared dimension tables to multiple fact tables, and linking 3 or more fact tables may produce unwanted results

Joins

When two tables, or data sets, contain the same key / identifier field, and you have the ability to join information in those tables together by linking that field. For example, we will spend a lot of time working with data from a fictitious Superstore company. The data contains order details for a variety of office supply products. There is a product identifier for every product sold. We can use this product identifier to match product details from a product table to order details in a sales table.

Think of a join as adding columns to a table, whenever the keys match.

Additionally, Tableau can combine tables or data sets containing the exact same columns, using a union. For example, if you had a table that was created monthly with the same 10 fields, unioning the data from 12 consecutive months would compile a data set for the entire year.

While the primary purpose of a join is to add columns, a union appends rows of information to the data.

Here is the summary from the Tableau website on joins and unions:

Join Type	Result	Description
Inner	When you use an inner join to combine tables, the result is a table that contains values that have matches in both tables.	
Left	When you use a left join to combine tables, the result is a table that contains all values from the left table and corresponding matches from the right table.	
	When a value in the left table doesn't have a corresponding match in the right table, you see a null value in the data grid.	
Right	When you use a right join to combine tables, the result is a table that contains all values from the right table and corresponding matches from the left table.	
	When a value in the right table doesn't have a corresponding match in the left table, you see a null value in the data grid.	
Full outer	When you use a full outer join to combine tables, the result is a table that contains all values from both tables.	
	When a value from either table doesn't have a match with the other table, you see a null value in the data grid.	
Union	Though union is not a type of join, union is another method for combining two or more tables by appending rows of data from one table to another. Ideally, the tables that you union have the same number of fields, and those fields have matching names and data types.	

Join types taken from Tableau Website

Tableau can also blend data together. When two data sources have unrelated, or loosely related data, Tableau has the ability to use them in them both visualizations. We will cover blends in more detail after joins and unions. However, it is important to note that the new relationships approach extends the power of blending data considerably.

Add a join

Data is often split into related tables for easier access and storage. Sometimes the related tables are worksheets in a spreadsheet, separate text files on a data lake, or modelled tables in a database. Tableau connects to any of those data source options, and is able to join data from multiple data sources and types. For databases and servers, you will need to add a connection to the server before you are able to see the tables.

We covered the data canvas and join editor above, but if you are using an earlier version of Tableau, your view will look like the following picture.

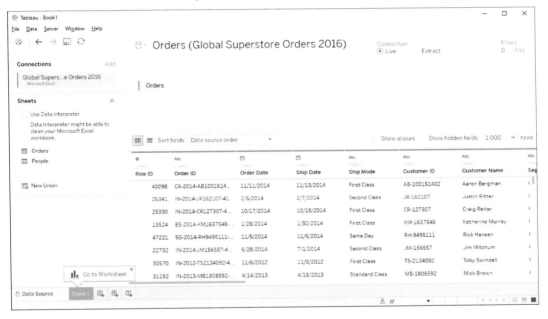

Data Connection 2020.1

Now that there is data for orders, we can connect Tableau to the second, ".csv" file, containing the returns data. There are two possible methods for adding the additional connection.

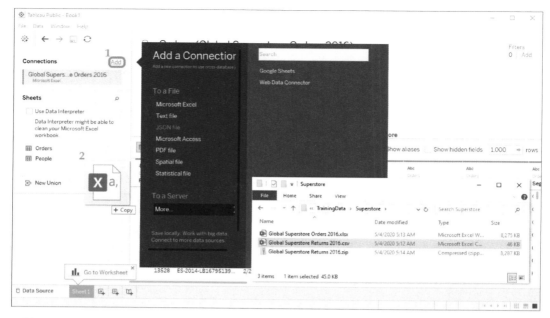

Add Connection

1. Using the "Add a Connection" menu, we can select the file, or server, type and follow the prompts.

2. We can drag the file from its folder into the Tableau workspace.

When we add the ".csv" file, Tableau will produce a default join or relationship between orders and returns. Tableau will automatically join datasets using field names with identical names.

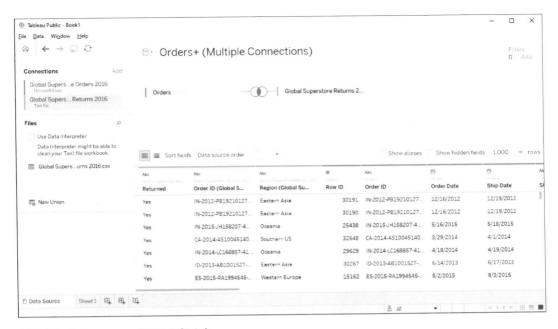

Multiple data sources 2020.1 (Join)

Additionally, notice that one connection has a blue accent and the other orange. This indicates the primary and secondary data. The coloring appears to the left of the connections in the connections pane, on the left side of the tables, and above the columns in the preview pane. The default join type is an inner join. Let's pop over to "Sheet 1" to look at the row count.

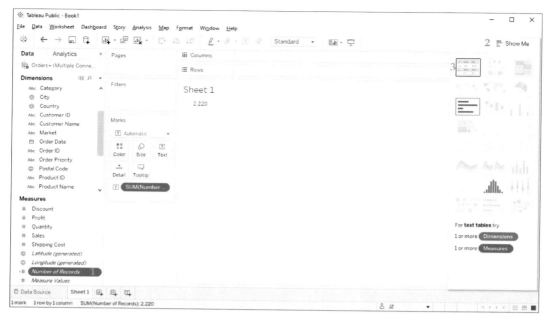

Inner Join Output

1. Select the "Number of Records" field in the data pane.

2. Click the "Show Me" button to display different chart options.

3. Click the data table.

We can see here that there are only 2,220 sales. That seems a low for a Global Superstore across multiple years. Perhaps it has to do with the join type. Returning to the "Data Source" tab, we can change the default join performed by Tableau.

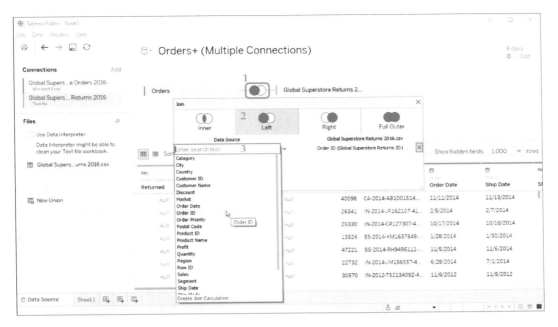

Joining data

1. Clicking the join icon brings up the join editor, and here you specify the join type and fields.

2. Click left join.

3. In the event that you do not have identical field names, this is where you click to manually specify the join fields.

After switching to a left join, you will notice that the total number of rows on "Sheet 1" is now 51,290. There were 51,290 orders during the period, but only 2,220 returns.

Experiment with the different join types to see the different outcomes, and for more information about joining tables, read the comprehensive explanation from the Tableau website[8], along with a link to their video lesson[9].

Add a union

When using two data sources with the identical column structures, it is possible to append the rows from each source into one complete data source. In SQL terms, this is a union. To follow along grab the rainfall data from the companion website.

The data consists two files from the Australian Bureau of Meteorology that contain daily rainfall measurements. The measurements correspond to recorded values at the Sydney Botanic Gardens during 2018 and 2019. To see the rainfall over both years as a continuous series, we need to union the data.

Connect to the 2018 file, and then there are two ways to union the 2019 data.

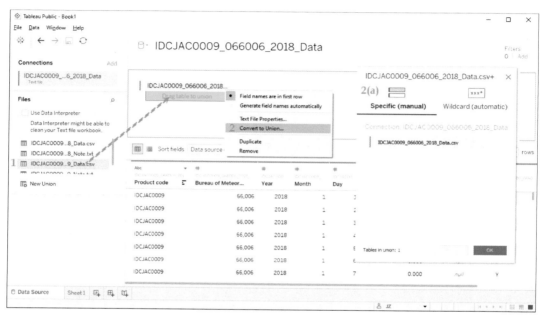

Union data

1. Drag the 2019 file to the data space until the orange union rectangle appears under the 2018 connection.

2. Use the table's drop-down menu to convert the table connection to a union. (If there is already a union established, the drop-down option is "Edit Union.")

    a. Drag the files to the union editor or use the wildcard union.

The first method works well when there are only one or two files to union. The second method is useful for a folder filled with files, and when there will be new files added to the folder, or server, location.

In our example, we only have the two files for 2018 and 2019, but if we had a folder with rainfall for every year from 1950, option 2 is more efficient. The files would likely have the same name with different years on the end, so the wildcard union is more efficient.

In computer terminology the asterisk ("*") character commonly serves as a wildcard in string searches. This means that when Tableau searches for files, it will match the specified text, and it will treat any string of characters as a match for an asterisk. For example, using "IDCJAC0009_066006*.csv" Tableau will match every file that starts with the specified string and ends with CSV.

In our example of files from 1950 - 2019, Tableau can automatically scan for the folder based on a wildcard string, and union all 69 files automatically. Additionally, Tableau will scan for and include any new files in the folder, whenever it refreshes the data connection.

Finally, the "New Union" button appears when the data source supports unions, and it uses the union editor to specify the union details. Then it adds the unioned tables as a new table, joining to any existing tables in the connection workspace.

For more information about Tableau and unions, here is a link to a comprehensive explanation from the Tableau website[10].

To recreate this rainfall union, download the sample data from the Zero to Data Viz site.

Add a blend

Blending data uses data from two different sources without joining the data together. Since the data calculations independently, blends are a great way to bring in reference data in Tableau, such as benchmarks, market performance, and other external information.

For example, suppose you want to know the market sizing for your Coffee Chain sales, and you want to compare it with sales at Office City, an office supply superstore. In this example the primary focus is sales at your coffee chain, and the Office City sales are supplemental information. Perhaps you want to partner with Office City, or maybe open your next Coffee Chain in the same parking lot.

To start you connect to the first data source, "Coffee Chain."

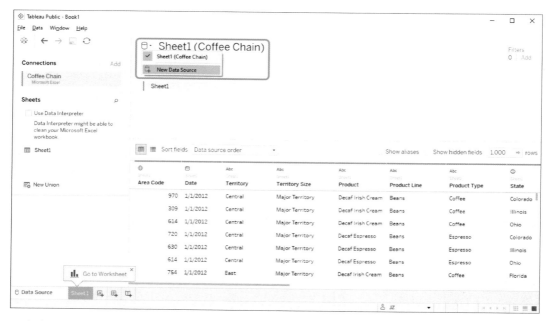

Including additional data sources from data source tab

Blending requires multiple data sources, and we can load these from both the data source (pictured above) and worksheet tabs (pictured below). On the data source tab, click the drop-down menu next to the data source icon, and select "New Data Source." This brings up the "New Data Source" connection interface, which follows the same connection process outlined earlier in section 2.

The process is similar from the worksheet, with two options for adding the connection.

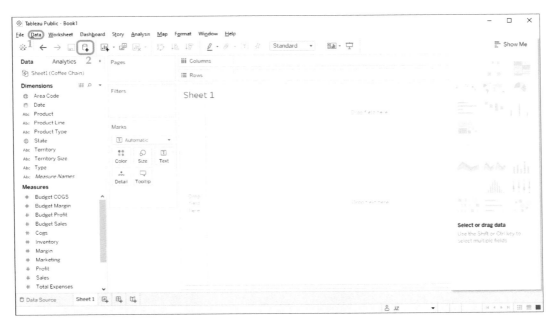

Additional data source from worksheet

1. Click the "Data" drop-down menu from the menubar, and select "New Data Source."

2. Click the "New Data Source" button in the toolbar.

Both the toolbar button and data menu, bring up the connection interface direct in the worksheet, and you follow the process to connect to data through the connection interface. After following this process to connect the "Office City" data, we can blend the information between both data sources.

Tableau blends the two data sources through fields with common values, like city or state. This produces independently aggregated values, and displays them based on common links. Put another way, Tableau runs two queries, one for each data source, and then it links the results based on a common field.

Tableau infers relationships for these linked fields, when the field names are identical. You can also specify data source relationships manually, from the data menu. To begin with, let's look at sales by state.

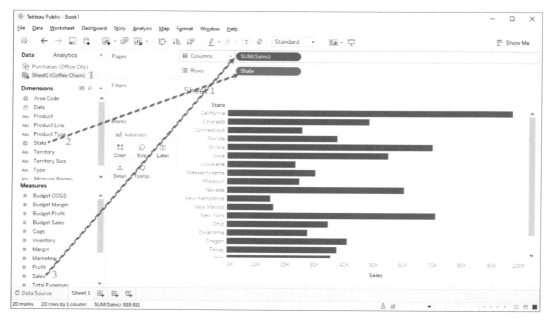

First Blend Source

1. Select the Coffee Chain data source.

2. Drag the state dimension to the rows shelf.

3. Drag the sales measure to the columns shelf

In our example, Coffee Chain is the primary focus, so we add it first. Tableau treats the first data source used as the primary data source for the worksheet. Tableau will display all results from the primary data set, and only the results from the secondary set that have a match for the linked fields.

This means that when we add the Office City sales, Tableau excludes the additional states that have Office City sales and no Coffee Chain sales. Tableau limits the display of linked fields based on values present in the primary source. For this reason, we only add state from the coffee chain data source.

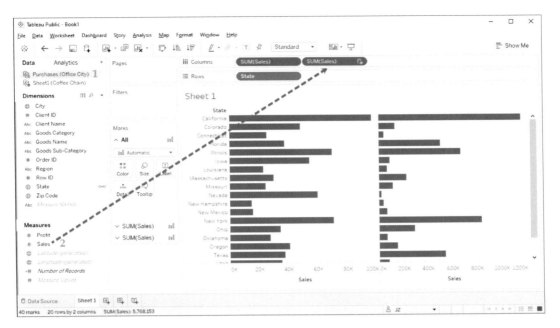

Second Blend Source

1. Select the Office City data source.

2. Drag sales to the columns shelf.

Since our data sets have identical field names for the link between them, the blend occurs automatically.

Now we can see the blended data side by side! Notice the list of states remains the same, despite Office City having sales in far more states than the Coffee Chain. Tableau uses the state dimension to link between the two data sources, and Tableau limits the results based on the states dimension from the primary data set.

In some cases, the linked fields may have different names, or fields with the same names may have different values. As mentioned previously, when the field names are identical Tableau automatically establishes the relationship link between sources and places an orange link icon next to the field. Clicking the link icon toggles the link on and off.

It is also possible to establish manual links and edit the default relationships, using the "Edit Blend Relationships menu.

Edit Relationships

1. Select "Edit Blend Relationships" from the Data drop-down menu in the menubar.

2. Click custom to add an additional field or edit the automatic match.

3. Click Add to bring up the field mapping interface.

4. Select the fields to link, and click "OK."

Both data sources have the same values for Territory and Region, so we can link them together for additional blending options. However, take a minute to do some analysis because that states don't necessarily map to the same region and territory in both data sources.

Finally, let's review the visual cues that Tableau provides when blending data.

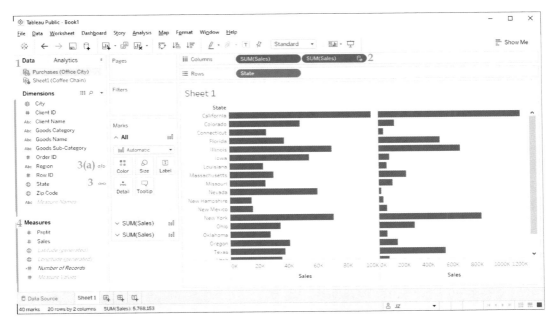

Blended Data

1. There is a blue check mark on the primary data source and an orange check on the secondary source.

2. The same icon appears on the Office City sales pill in the columns shelf.

3. There are link icons next to fields with established relationships.

a. Grey indicates an unused link, and orange indicates an active link.

4. Tableau includes an orange line on the left edge of the dimensions and measure panes to indicate the secondary data source selection.

As a reminder, the primary and secondary designations are sheet specific, and Tableau determines the primary source based on the first source added to the viz.

To wrap up, the two primary uses of blending are reference data such as sales goals, or project team groupings that don't align to account team structures. Blends are also useful for combining external data with your companies internal data sources.

In most corporations, the data sources are database servers. Databases require an architectural design, and controls to ensure the data is accurate. Typically, there is a small team of IT professionals with privileges to make changes to this type of data warehouse. These IT teams are usually in very high demand.

Goals and project teams can change rapidly, and it may not make sense from a priority or timing perspective to engage IT. This is where Tableau's ability to blend data is helpful. The project management team can manage a spreadsheet with current goals and team members, and we can blend the database and spreadsheet information seamlessly with Tableau.

Additionally, external information like weather patterns, economic factors, and other public data sets help provide market and environmental context to internal company data. Since we have no control over the structure of these external data sources, blending the data in Tableau lets analysts include the information without the cost or wait time of loading it into a data warehouse.

To learn more, Tableau has a video[11] on data blending.

To read more about blending data, here is the comprehensive explanation from the Tableau website[12].

Manage data properties

Setting the data properties correctly dramatically increases the efficiency of your workflow in Tableau. This does not change the underlying data, but it ensures Tableau interprets and displays the data correctly.

You can manage data properties from both the data source tab and the data pane in the worksheet. There are also view-specific properties available when you select pills in the worksheet cards and shelves.

Before we start managing data properties, we need to have an idea of the values the data contains. The "Describe" feature is a great way to view a summary of a field's metadata.

Describe Field

1. Right-click the Territory field from our blending example, and there is an option at the bottom of the drop-down menu to "Describe" the field.

2. Clicking describe opens the "Describe Field" box, with details about the field and its contents. (Note for fields with a lot of different values, you can use the load button to view additional values.)

Using the describe feature is helpful when connecting to data for the first time, and it available in the data source tab and worksheet, when you right-click a field. The Describe Field window provides helpful information for managing the data properties of specific fields.

Rename a data field

Knowing that territory matches the region field from our Office City data, we can rename the territory field so that Tableau automatically picks up the link relationship.

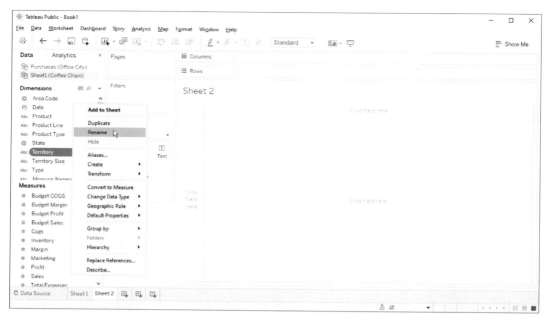

Rename data field

Right-click the Territory field, and select "Rename" from the drop-down menu. A cursor will appear on the field in the side-bar, and you can type in the new name. You can also perform a slow double click on the field to bring up the cursor. Both methods work in the worksheet and the data source tab.

In our example, renamed the field so it matched the name in another data set. You will also need to rename fields for the following reasons: * field names are cryptic due to abbreviation * field names contain lots of underscores or dashes * when database column names Other reasons you want to rename fields, are when the database field names are a bit cryptic, contain lots of underscores, contain typos, or you simply want to match the current vocabulary of the business for a more polished presentation of information.

It is important to note that Tableau uses the renamed field to create calculated fields, which we will cover later in the book.

Assign an alias to a data value

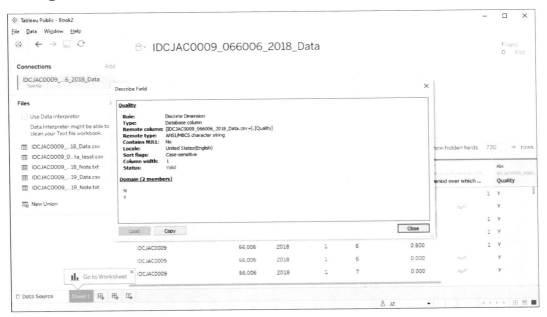

Original Quality Values

Tableau splits the fields into measures and dimensions, which we cover in the next section on understanding Tableau concepts. Measures are easily aggregated numeric fields, and dimensions are descriptive fields. There tend to be a fixed number of different values for a dimension, like in the Quality field from the rain measurements. There are two members in the quality dimension, Y and N.

An alias changes the display value of a dimension member, without impacting the underlying data. For example, quality values Y and N indicate the rain measurement was Quality Assured or Not Quality Assured, respectively.

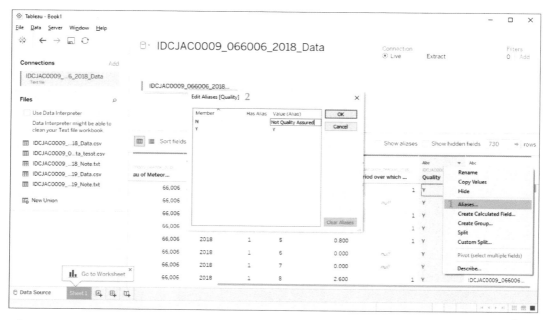

Alias Menu

1. Right-click the field, and select the "Aliases" option.

2. Use the "Edit Aliases" interface to alias the values for Y and N.

Once we alias the dimension's member values, Tableau displays the aliased value instead of the original data. Unlike renaming a field, the alias values are superficial. When using a field with aliases in joins, or calculations, Tableau processes the underlying queries using the original values. In our example, Tableau would use the "Y" and "N" values.

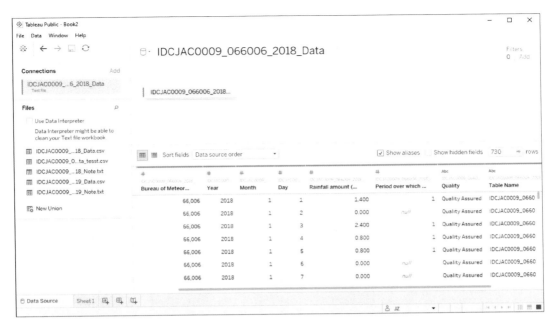

Aliased Quality Values

The alias menu is available both in the data source tab and viz worksheet's data pane, and it only applies to dimensions.

Assign a geographic role to a data field

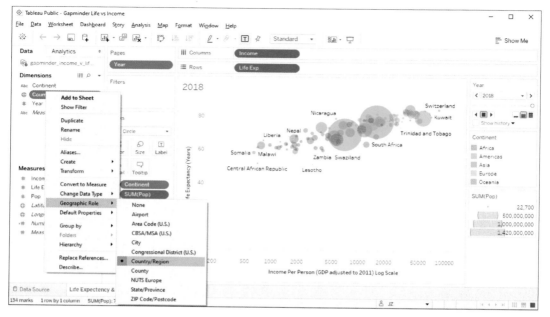

Geographic Role

In the "Office City" data set used in the blending example, notice the little globe icon next to the city, state, and zip code fields. This indicates that the field is a geographic location, and as such, is mappable. Tableau has the capability to display information on a geographic map using these fields. Simple right-click on the field, highlight "Geographic Role," and then select the correct role (e.g.. City, County, Country/Region).

On the data source tab there is a data type icon for each column, and it provides another way to specify its geographic role. Clicking the icon brings up the drop-down menu to specify the field's data type, and selecting the menu item for geographic role displays the available geographic roles.

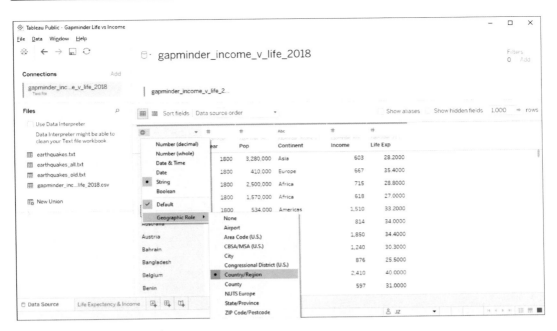

Geographic Role - Data Tab

Change data type for a data field (number, date, string, Boolean, etc.)

Beyond the mechanics of setting data types, note that you need to set the data types before you create a Tableau extract. The data types determine rounding and other treatments during Tableau's calculations, and you may notice discrepancies based on the precision of decimals or other factors.

Tableau data types and their icons:

Icon	Data type
Abc	Text (string) values
🗓	Date values
🗓	Date & Time values
#	Numerical values
T|F	Boolean values (relational only)
⊕	Geographic values (used with maps)
🖳	Cluster Group (used with Find Clusters in Data ⬛)

Tableau provides the data type settings in both the data source tab and the view worksheet. Click the data type icon in the data source tab, or right-click the field in the data pane of the worksheet to bring up the "Change Data Type" menu.

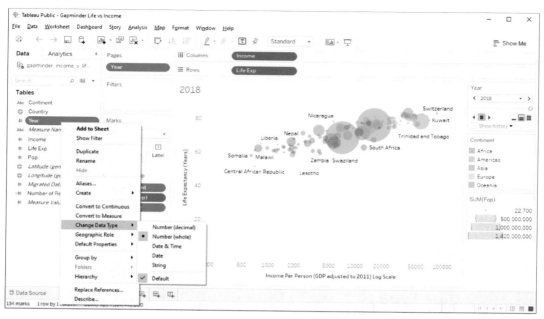

Change Data Type - Worksheet

As mentioned Tableau's behavior changes based on the data type. This is important when considering any missing (null) value and when fields contain multiple data types in the same column. For example, there might be a string field that contains numeric or date values.

Dates and numbers in a string field show as text. For date fields, text is treated as a null value, and numbers are treated as the day in the sequence starting with 01/01/1900 represented as 0. To clarify different software and programming languages tend to use numeric values to represent dates, but they may use different starting points. For Tableau, 0 is January 1, 1900, 1 is January 2, 1900, and it continues. In this system January 1, 2000 is 36527.

The inverse is true of dates in a numeric field. There the date will show up as the numeric value from the sequence. This means that January 1, 2000 shows up as 36527 in a numeric field.

For Boolean fields, Tableau treats non-Boolean values as null.

Change default properties for a data field (number format, aggregation, color, date format, etc.)

Tableau includes the ability to tweak he default treatment of fields. This is especially handy when reusing a data source across teams and reports because you can set consistent colors throughout. For example, in the Gapminder data we can specify the default colors for each continent. Wherever continent is used the coloring will be consistent, and users will know red indicates values for Asia.

For measures, you can set default properties for comment, color, number format, aggregation, and "total using." Default properties help with consistency throughout a workbook, and this improves the readability of visualizations for your audience. For example, the comments let you provide a brief field description when hovering, which reduces the need for a separate data dictionary, and enables additional context.

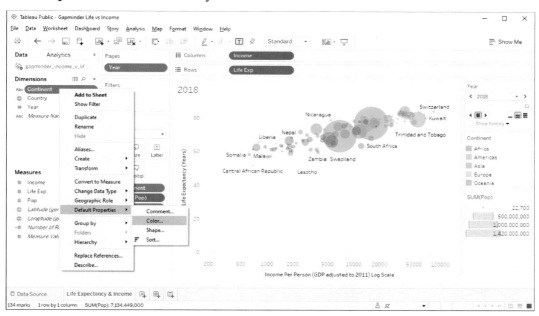

Changing default properties

To set default properties, right-click a field in the data side-bar of the worksheet, and hover the mouse cursor over "Default Properties." The menu then displays the available default properties for the field type.

All Fields

- *Comment* determines what displays in the tooltips, when a user hovers the mouse over a data field pill in the data pane or elsewhere in the tableau application.

- *Color* specifies the default color or color range for a field. * *Number Format* this specifies how a numeric field displays in the workbook, for example the number of decimal places, commas, and more.

Dimensions

- *Shape* assigns a specific mark shape to a dimension member when the visualization uses shapes.

- *Sort* sets the default sort order for the field.

Measures

- *Aggregation* specifies which aggregation Tableau uses when adding the measure in the workbook, for example sum, mean, and more.

- *Total Using* specifies the aggregation used when totalling the field.

For dimensions, you can add a default comment that displays when the mouse hovers above the field, default color, default shape, and default sort. If the dimension is numeric, there is an option for setting the default number properties.

Extracts and Saving Connections

You will need a cursory understanding of live connections and extracts, and these options are only available in the fully licensed Tableau Desktop software. We cover an overview here, and you should revisit this section during your free trial period.

Live connections vs Extracts

When you select your data source in the connection pane, Tableau brings up a preview of the data, along with any additional tables you can join. Tableau can run queries against the live data source, or it can extract data from the source into it's proprietary Tableau Hyper extract format. The extract contains optimization for the way Tableau processes its internal query engine.

Tableau executes queries against the data source to assemble information for the visualizations. A live data source connection ensures visualization contains the most up to date information from the data source. A Tableau extract contains a point-in-time snapshot of the data.

While using a live connection provides current, or potentially real-time, data, there is a performance trade off. Tableau relies on the external data for executing the queries, and depending on the data source, performance may be significantly slower than the extract. This impacts the viewers experience because the dashboards and visualizations will take longer to load when they adjust filters or other interactive elements.

Conversely, a Tableau Data Extract provides a snapshot of the data stored on your local hard drive, or the server for published reports. Tableau loads the extract into memory as needed to produce the visualization. You can create an extract from a local file (.csv, .xlsx, .txt, etc..), or from a database, and either way it usually speeds up the performance.

The exception is when you have a powerful enough database that is properly tuned because the database will likely manipulate the data faster than the Tableau engine. This is especially relevant when working with extremely large datasets. Beyond 500,000 rows, Tableau begins to struggle with some calculations.

For more context, a database is a collection of tables that contain related data. When multiple tables have the same field, like a customer ID value, then you can join those tables together to get information related to a specific customer ID from all of the tables with the ID. Most databases, especially ones that are not deployed on cloud technology, process joining and analyzing tables using the data from the hard disk. More powerful, modern databases use an in-memory engine. This in-memory processing pulls the data into the system's memory (RAM), which allows it to work with the data much faster. With computers, memory is typically faster than hard disks.

Tableau's internal process engine runs in-memory so using a Tableau data extract tends to provide better performance. Generally speaking, it is best to use extracts most of the time and save the live connections special circumstances when the data updates more frequently, like stock prices. With a live connection, every viewer interaction fires off multiple queries, which can result in slower performance depending on network traffic, database processing power, and other capacity factors.

Tableau's Hyper extracts are shared either as part of a packaged workbook (.twbx) or packaged data source (.tdsx).

Create an extract

As mentioned above, Tableau Public does not include the live connection feature, and creates an extract by default to publish the workbook to your Tableau Public profile. This is one of the key differences between desktop and public. With Tableau Desktop, you can create proprietary Tableau data file that speeds up Tableau's processing.

While you are unable to do this with Tableau Public, you need a cursory understanding of how it works, in case it comes up as a multiple choice question on the exam.

When using Tableau Desktop, you there are two ways to create an extract. The first is to click the extract radio button on the data source tab of the worksheet.

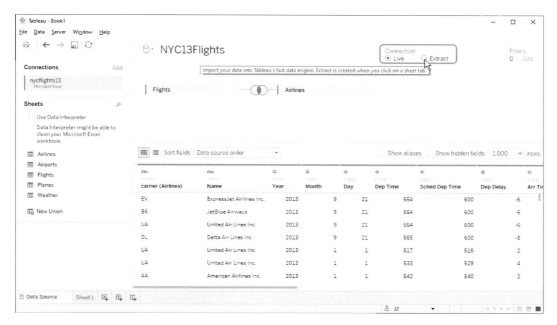

Create an Extract from the data interface

Hovering the mouse over the "Extract" radio button causes Tableau to present a tooltip with a message that the extract will be created when you click on the sheet tab. When you move to the worksheet, Tableau brings up a save extract dialogue box, and you can specify the extract file name and location.

If you want to have more control over extract settings, or if you decide to switch after working with the data, there is also an extract option from the Tableau worksheet.

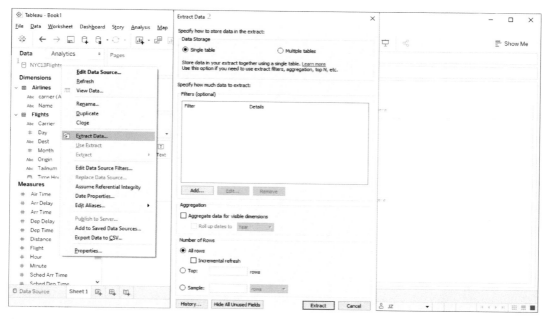

Create an Extract from the worksheet

1. Right-click on the data source from within the worksheet / authoring interface and select extract data.

2. The "Extract Data" interface appears.

With this method, there are more extract options. This is where you can apply data source filters for the extract, use default aggregation to reduce the number of rows, and restrict the number of rows in the extract. To restrict the number of rows, you can choose to set a row limit, return the top N number of rows, and for some data sources use a random sample of records.

Additionally, creating the extract this way allows you to specify a single table or multiple tables extract. There are a series of conditions that must be met to use a multiple table extract, and you only want to use it when the single table extract produces more records than expected.

The multiple table extract also requires that certain conditions be met within the data source.

- Multiple table extracts require all joins to be inner joins, or equality joins

- The data types for any join columns are the same across tables

- There are no pass-through SQL queries

- Incremental refresh is off

- There are no extract filters

- The Sampling and Top N number of rows features are off

Creating the extract from the data source tab produces a default, single-table extract.

Save metadata in a .tds

Saving a TDS file is another feature that is exclusive to Tableau Desktop.

Once you finish connecting to your data and managing the data properties, it is helpful to save the metadata in a ".tds" file, especially if you or your colleagues will reuse this data connection across different projects or workbooks. When using Tableau Desktop, you can save the ".tds" file locally, on your Tableau Server, or using Tableau Online.

The information that you input regarding the relationships, data types, and column names is "metadata." Metadata is information that describes data, and Tableau can store this information as a .tds file. The TDS file contains the relevant metadata associated with a data connection, so all users of the data source are able to quickly connect to the data without having to redo the data preparation.

Here is a list of metadata / changes that Tableau saves in the .tds file:

- Folder groupings - for data sets with a large number of fields, it is possible to group the fields into folders for easier navigation

- Renamed fields

- Data types

- Calculated variables

- Sets

- Groups

- Hierarchies

- Default properties, such as aggregation, totals, number / date formatting, colors, and comments

Saving a TDS file

To save a .tds files, start in the one of the worksheets, also known as the authoring interface. Right-click the data source, and select "Add to Saved Data Sources" in the drop-down menu. Connections saved as .tds files in the default local location show up at the bottom of the connections pane under saved connections, and you only have to make those edits once. The saved data source will appear in the bottom corner

Understanding Tableau Concepts

Learning Outcome

Tableau's approach to data focuses on streamlining the visualization process, and it provides immense flexibility. The core concepts in this section are the building blocks data visualization with Tableau, and a high-level understanding is essential before tackling more complex features and capabilities.

By the end of this section you will understand:

- that dimensions typically provide qualitative information that describes the quantitative values contained within measures

- how Tableau displays discrete (blue pills) and continuous (green pills) data in the worksheets

- how and why tableau aggregates measures into summary information about the data set

- the parts of the worksheet that drive the visualization's level of detail (Viz LOD) and how the questions asked drive the level of detail

Dimensions and measures

After setting up the data, Tableau will take you to a worksheet to start building visualizations. On left side of the window, the data pane contains the data source fields, and there are two sections, dimensions and measures. Dimensions are on the top containing the descriptive fields, and measures are on the bottom, containing the easily aggregated numerical fields.

Explain what kind of information dimensions usually contain

Dimensions typically contain qualitative information, such as names, dates, demographics, and geography, and most commonly dimensions are discrete values.

Explain what kind of information measures usually contain

Measures are commonly quantitative information that is easily aggregated with standard descriptive statistics. Measures often include prices, volumes, scientific readings, and other continuous values.

Discrete and continuous fields

As mentioned above, dimensions tend to be discrete values ("individually separate and distinct"), while measures tend to be continuous values ("forming an unbroken whole").

A discrete field contains a specific set of values, regardless of type (numeric, string, or date). A continuous field an infinite number of possible values, and it is either numeric or a continuous date. Stock symbol is a common example of a discrete value, and the stock's price is continuous. As another example think of lending products. Type (home loan, credit card, personal loan, etc.) is discrete, while the interest rate is continuous.

As a final example, consider a person's age. Stored as an integer, representing fixed lifespan, age is discrete. Represented as bins ("25-29") age is also discrete. However, represented as a decimal value based on time in existence, age becomes continuous. An age of 25.6 is 25 years and six month, 9,344 days, or 224,256 hours. This ability to further divide the age into smaller and smaller fractions between values makes it continuous.

Discrete variables are typically categorical, descriptive values like gender, marital status, and education level, and continuous variables are numerical values like stock prices, interest rates, temperatures, and other "measurement" values.

Explain how discrete and continuous fields are displayed in Tableau

Most often, discrete fields are dimensions and continuous fields are measures; however, that is not always the case. In the image below notice the green year pill. Typically, year is a discrete field, but for illustrative purposes it presents here as discrete in the pages card and continuous in the dimensions pane.

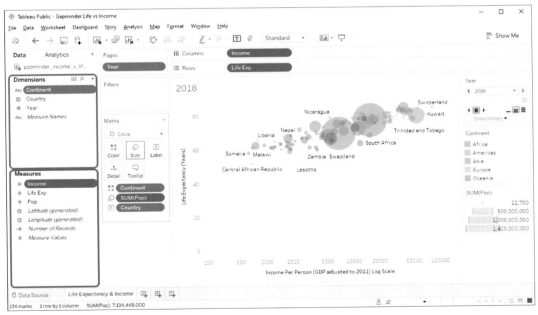

Dimensions and Measures

Discrete measures and dimensions appear in Tableau as blue pills. Continuous measures and dimension appear in Tableau as green pills. By default, Tableau aggregates measures, as you see with the sum of population in the marks card. However, for this graph, I converted the income and life expectancy fields to dimensions, which is why they are not aggregated. They still show as green because they are continuous fields.

In Tableau, discrete fields create headers in the worksheet, while continuous fields create axes. This is a good way to think of discrete versus continuous values, with respect to creating views. When adding color and other aesthetics to a view, Tableau responds differently continuous and discrete values. For example, dropping continuous fields onto color in the marks card produces a shaded color range, while a discrete value simply colors the marks differently for each of the discrete values, like the bubbles in the Gapminder visual.

Additionally, the data type icons are blue for discrete fields and green for continuous fields. This is consistent across the view worksheet and the data source tab.

As a final note, Tableau also displays continuous and discrete fields differently across components of a viz. For example, a continuous x-axis displays bars that touch, whereas a discrete horizontal axis leaves space between the bars. Another example is color, which shows continuous fields as a range of color, while discrete values have individual colors assigned to them. We cover these in more detail as we progress through the book.

Explain the difference between discrete date parts and continuous date values in Tableau

Tableau's presentation of dates is extremely flexible, and a thorough understanding is essential. While most fields in a data source are either discrete or continuous, dates are both.

Right-click a date field in one of the shelves or cards, and Tableau presents the drop-down menu pictured below. I added markings to denote discrete vs. continuous date parts.

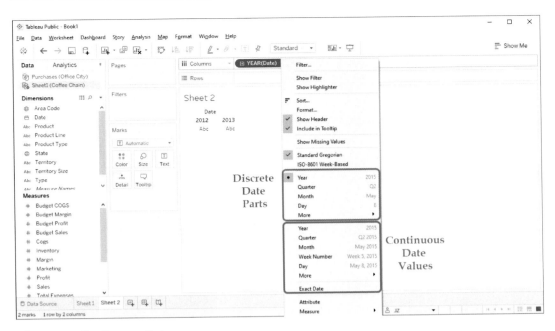

Discrete vs. Continuous Dates

Viewing a single part of the date provides a discrete value, such day of the week. While they are sequential, there are 7 distinct, possible values (Monday to Sunday). In the image above, the blue box contains discrete values, while the green box represents continuous date values.

Continuous date values focus on the time aspect a date. Using time, we are able to divide time into infinitely smaller segments, year, month, day, hour, second, and it continues.

Additionally Tableau provides a default hierarchy on date fields. We will cover more on hierarchies in a later section. For now, just know that the plus symbol on a date pill pops out a second pill with the next interval. Clicking the plus icon on YEAR(date) pops out QUARTER(date), and the minus icon will collapse all the nested pills. I marked these icons in the image below.

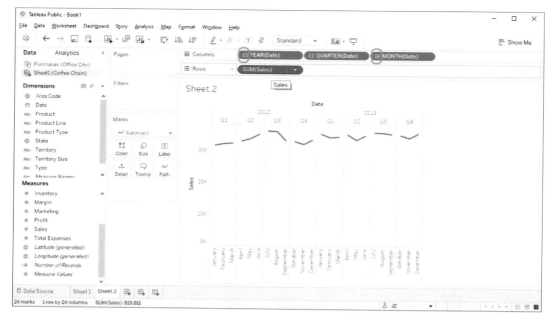

Discrete Dates

Tableau defaults the chart type to a line graph, when there is a date on the x-axis (columns shelf). Looking at the chart above, notice how the line is broken up into discrete parts. There is a mark for each month, separated into a quarter, and then the quarters are broken up by year. There are 2 years, 8 quarters, or 24 months displayed.

If we remove the year and quarter pills from the shelf, then Tableau will aggregate by month only.

Discrete Date Aggregation

Despite the aggregation of sales including values from both 2012 and 2013, Tableau only displays 12 months because the above chart no longer includes the year dimension.

Using the continuous month value, the graph displays 24 months.

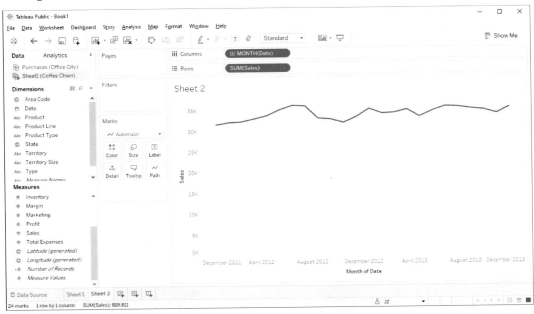

Continuous Dates

As a final note on discrete versus continuous dates, Tableau treats them differently, with respect to including marks in the view. Discrete date values only show dates present in the data set, whereas continuous date values will show all dates, irrespective of the values in the data set. For example, if you have daily stock prices for March 1st to 31st, the continuous date will include every day from 1 to 31, and if there is no price on the 8th, Tableau includes the eighth with a zero value. Conversely, for a discrete date value, Tableau omits the 8th entirely.

Aggregation

In Tableau, it is possible to aggregate numerical values, regardless of whether the value is a dimension or measure. However, it is far more common to aggregate measures.

Aggregation uses mathematical operations to summarize individual data points into clusters of information. The classic example is aggregating a student's class performance into an average across all the exams, quizzes and assignments. The sum of the scores divided by the number scores recorded equals the average. This combines multiple scores into a single score per student, which we can further aggregate into a score the entire class. In tableau the student identifier and class names are dimensions.

Using the dimensions, Tableau aggregates information across different levels of detail. Unless specified, a sum is the default aggregation used by Tableau. Let's load the Global Superstore data, and work through an example.

Adding the Sales measure to the rows shelf produces a single bar for total Sales in the dataset. Adding dimensions segments the data into clusters of detail, for example sales by category, region or customer. Absent these dimension the total displayed is all superstore sales between 2012 and 2015.

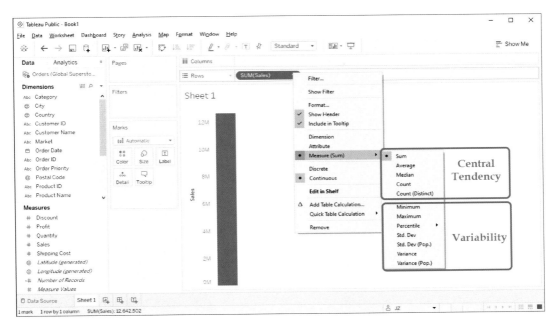

Aggregation

Right-clicking on the green pill for SUM(Sales), provides an option to change the measure's aggregation. The drop-down menu includes common descriptive statistics. Descriptive statistics primarily measure one of two things, central tendency (mean, median, and mode) or variability (range, minimum, maximum, variance, and standard deviation). The drop-down menu separates the aggregation options into those two groups that are more or less central tendency and variability. I include sum and count in the central tendency box because an average is the sum divided by the count.

Explain why Tableau aggregates measures

When adding a measure to a visualization, Tableau aggregates the field by default, and according to the official documentation, the "default aggregation applied varies depending on the context of the view." However, the most common default is the sum. There is no official explanation for why the sum is the most common default, but the broader Tableau community believes sum is the default because it is most commonly used. It is also worth noting that you can specify the default aggregation for fields in your data source, by following the steps to change a field's default properties (see Section 2).

The primary reason for aggregated measures is their ability to present layered details. The additional layers of information available through aggregated measures compared with disaggregated measures explain why it is the default behavior to aggregate measures. Consider, for example, sales.

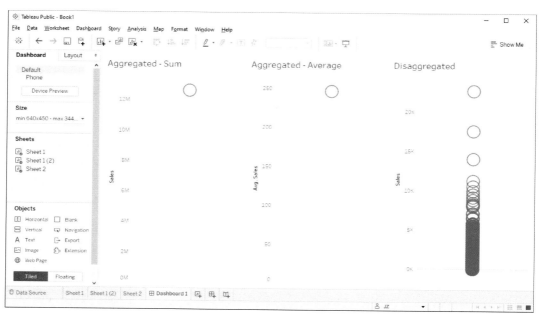

Aggregated vs. Disaggregated

While the scatter plot on the right provides some information, the overlapping points distort the ability to look at total sales. We can see in the disaggregated data on the right that we have some extremely large sales that sit as outliers toward the higher values, but the highest concentration of sales is down in the lower amounts. The aggregated values on the left provides the detail more precisely, faster, and with more flexibility to add additional detail through the various aesthetic layers of color, shape, and size.

On the left, it is easy to see that total sales are about 12.5 million, and the average sale amount is $245. Visualizations are supposed to leverage the ability of a picture to quickly tell a story, and aggregating measures is a great way to do that. We could even leverage dual or combined axis features to layer both the average and the sum on the same view. There are times when disaggregated measures are useful, such as scatter plots, but more often aggregated measure convey more information.

Describe how an aggregated measure changes when dimensions are added to the view

The dimensions allow us to layer in additional levels of detail with our aggregate measures. In the sales example above we can look at sales by order date, sales by category, or even both sales by order date and category.

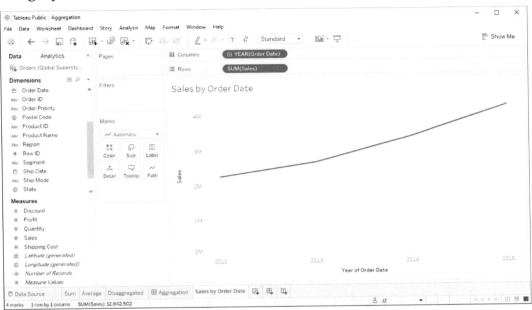

Sales by Order Date

Double-clicking the fields adds them using Tableau's default placement. Tableau automatically adds the summed Sales field to rows, and the year of the Order Date field to columns. The marks are set to automatic, so the visualization type changes to a line graph. Note that I changed the year value to a continuous date part improve the display of the line.

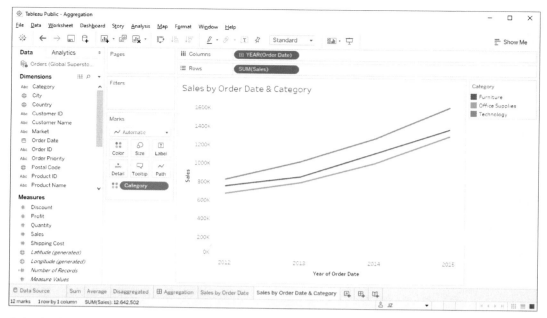

Sales by Category

Double-clicking the Category dimension, Tableau adds it to the chart. Typically, the default placement should be the color tile on the marks card, but the default placement varies based on the viz type and included fields.

Now, the visualization shows the sales in each category across the 4 years.

Combined with aggregated measures, dimensions segment the data into groups, and the aggregation is performed at the level of detail associated with the group. You can also use totals and calculations to layer different levels of detail within a viz.

Level of Detail

While it doesn't have its own heading in the outline of topics for the exam, level of detail is an essential concept in Tableau, and it is the core of why Tableau behaves differently based on where you drop dimension and measures.

The level of detail is driven by the questions asked of the data. For example:

- Can we flag all customers from January 2014, and use that to analyze sales to that particular cohort / vintage?

- Can we plot the largest sale in each region, and compare it to the average by market?

The first thing to understand is the source data. What is the grain at which the data is captured? The grain, or lowest level row detail, for the Superstore data set is the item level per order. The uniqueness of a row is set by a combination of "Order ID" and "Product ID."

From there, we can aggregate the data by order, categories, sales region, and other dimensions to visually explore the data at different levels of detail.

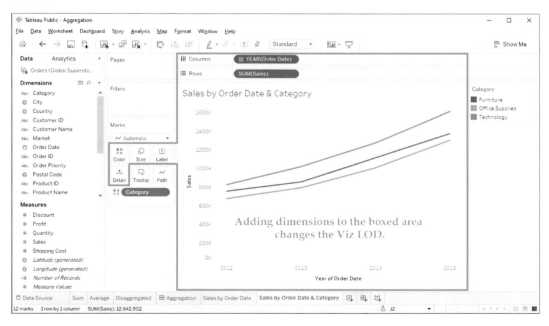

Visualization Level of Detail

Every time we add a dimension to an area in a blue box above, the data is aggregated to the "Viz LOD." In the graph above with Sales by Year and Category, the Viz LOD is Category and Year, and all aggregation rolls up to those two dimensions.

As you will see later in the book, Tableau also includes Level of Detail (LOD) expressions that function like a short-hand SQL, allowing you to layer levels of detail. These LOD expressions enable calculations to aggregate values independently of the visualization's LOD. That's enough detail for now, and we will dive deeper, later in the book.

As we begin to explore more advanced Tableau features, knowing the viz level of detail is the key to knowing how Tableau will calculate values and present the visual.

Exploring & Analyzing Data

Learning outcome

There are many ways to analyze data, from the simple use of Excel to writing complex machine learning algorithms in R or Python. Choosing the right tool is essential, and visualizing the data lets you quickly identify key trends and relationships. Visualizing data also makes quality issues more visible, and it adds efficiency to the often cumbersome data wrangling process.

By the end of this section you will understand:

- how and when to create each of the basic charts in Tableau

- how to make those charts interactive and dynamic using filters, groups and sets

- how to use calculations and analytics to enhance the explanatory power of data visualizations

- how to use parameters to provide interactive analysis to viewers

- the value of bins and histograms and the basic statistical concepts that drive this value

Create basic charts

The title "basic charts" undersells the importance of these graphics in visual storytelling. These simple charts are the foundation of data exploration, analysis, and insights. As the classic adage goes, "Simplicity is the ultimate sophistication."

When selecting data fields for analysis, Tableau produces certain chart types by default as you add fields into the worksheet, but that's just a starting point. As an analyst, you need to see past what is in front of you to evolve the visuals. Great data visualization packs in just enough information to tell the story, without distracting from the point. A useful question to ask yourself is, "What would I like to show, a comparison, composition, distribution or relationship?" Then, always follow-up with the question, "If I add this does it add clarity or distract from the message?" If it is a distraction don't bother cramming in the additional information.

Here are the primary types of charts and the most common reasons for selecting them in your visualization:

- **Line Charts** work well for tracking trends through time, especially when the changes between periods are smaller.

- **Bar Charts** are great for comparison between different groups and larger changes over time.

- **Scatter Plots** are an effective tool for examining the relationship between two variables.

- **Area Charts** are similar to line charts, but provide an option to show the parts of the whole through stacking and coloring.

- **Maps** are useful for comparing geographic areas, when there are geographic fields in the data set.

- **Pie Charts** show parts of a whole, but their one-dimensionality makes them an inefficient choice. (*You can show the same thing with a stacked bar graph and include additional dimensions.*)

There are three locations in the workbook that you can create a new chart / sheet, as well as a keyboard shortcut (Control + M or Command + M).

Create worksheet

1. Use the Worksheet drop-down menu in the menubar.

2. Use the new sheet button in the toolbar.

3. Use the new sheet button in the navigation tabs.

Create a standard and stacked bar chart

Bar charts are extremely versatile, and they are one of the most common visualizations. They are easy to read, and bar charts provide quick insight into comparisons, composition and distribution of data. The humble bar chart shows trends, differences, categorical comparisons, and more, at a glance.

There are three primary choices for an analyst to make on bar charts: 1) orientation (horizontal vs. vertical), 2) stacked vs. side-by-side, and 3) the use of color.

Orientation is driven by the type of fields in the columns and rows shelves. A single dimension on rows with a measure on columns, creates a horizontal bar chart. Swapping the placement of the dimension and measure creates a vertical bar chart. Time is always a vertical bar chart with dates and times on the x-axis, and Tableau tends to place aggregated measures on the y-axis.

Stacked bar charts are great when you want to see parts of the whole, and side-by-side bars are great for comparison between members of a dimension.

Coloring is a great way to easily identify dimension members throughout a workbook or dashboard, such as categories. If a category value has the same color everywhere it is easy to spot its metrics. For example, make the Furniture category show up as blue throughout the visuals, and every time the viewer sees blue they know it is furniture.

There are two ways to create a bar chart in Tableau. First we can use the "Show Me" menu. Notice in the image below, that some chart thumbnails in the "Show Me" Menu are faded out. Tableau only displays buttons for the charts that it can create with the currently selected fields. Hovering over these icons, the menu includes the required number of dimensions and measures to produce the visual.

Show Me - Bar chart

1. Holding the control key (command on a Mac), click to select a discrete dimension and the "Sales" measure.

2. Click the "Show Me" button.

3. Select the horizontal bar chart button.

Horizontal Bar Chart

Additionally, we can create a bar chart by dragging or double-clicking the dimensions and measures to place them on the columns and rows shelves.

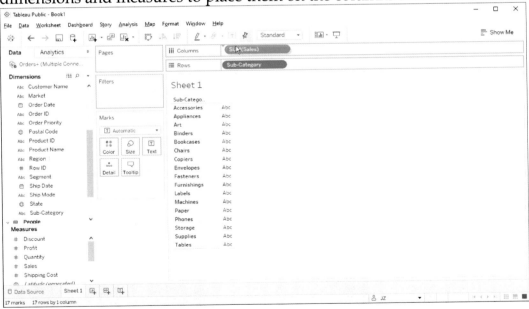

Drag / Double-Click Bar Chart

To create a vertical bar chart, swap the placement of Sub-category and Sales on the rows and columns shelves, as pictured below.

Vertical Bar Chart

With this particular visual notice the difference in readability between horizontal and vertical orientation. The sub-categories are easier to read in the horizontal orientation, and there is a slight difference in the details that standout regarding the bars. I notice the low points in the bars a little more with the vertical bars, and with the horizontal bars, the larger bars grab more attention.

Tableau can layer in the detail from "Category", by adding it as a second dimension.

2 Dimensions Bar Chart

Drag Category to the left of the Sub-category dimension, and Tableau segments the sub-category bars based on category. We can even take it a step further and add the order date to include a time element. Note that Tableau displays the panes differently based on the pill order in the shelf.

Bar Chart Trend

While we can see the leading sub-categories through time, the chart becomes messy, and now, it extends beyond the window. Tableau provides a scroll bar to see the remaining portion of the graph, but this creates extra work for the viewer.

As an alternative, we layer in thethe sub-categories using a different aesthetic, like color. Let's go through the process, which will highlight how Tableau makes assumptions based on the types of fields and their placement on the worksheet. Tableau will change the mark type, and we will change it back.

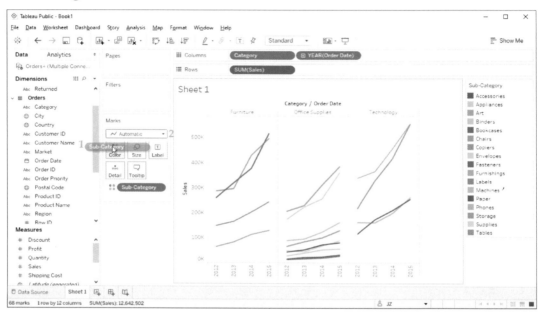

Dragging Sub-category to Color

1.   Dag the Sub-category pill to the Color tile on the Marks card.

2.   Notice how the marks drop-down changed from a bar icon next to the work Automatic to a line icon, and the graph now shows lines. Click the drop-down and select "Bar" to change it back.

Stacked Bar Chart

Much better! Now, we have a stacked bar chart. Stacked bar charts quickly show the composition of value by different segments so we can see the largest subcategories by sales. This graph quickly illustrates the category and sub-category relationship, the growth in sales by both of those dimensions through the 4 years in the data, and it fits concisely in the window. This graph has room for stylistic improvements, but for now, let's advance through to scatter plots.

Create a scatter plot

Scatter plots display two variables along the x and y axes, and this view highlights the relationship between the two variables. When the two variables are correlated they will move in a consistent direction, often implying the shape of a positive or negative sloping diagonal line. Positive indicates that the two variables move together in the same direction, and negative indicates that they move in opposite directions. For example, let's look at the 2019 summer temperatures in Dallas / Ft. Worth, Texas. In this first graph we will plot the daily high in Fahrenheit along the y-axis and Celsius along the x-axis.

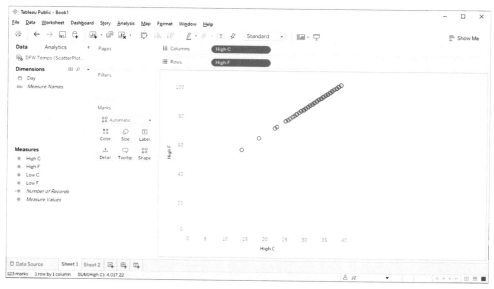

Celsius vs. Fahrenheit Temps

The upward sloping diagonal line demonstrates positive correlation, and in this case, the values are perfectly correlated because they are different scales to represent the same temperature. As the Fahrenheit temperature increases, the Celsius temperature increases in equal proportion.

If we plot the daily high against the daily low, we expect to see an upward sloping line, but the correlation will not be perfect because the high and low temps do not change from day to day by the same amount.

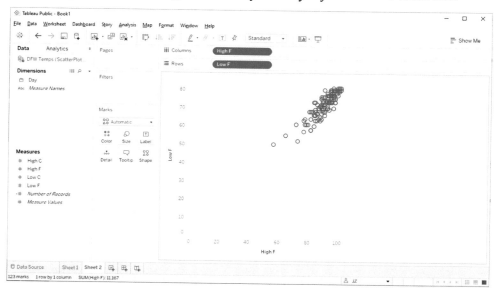

High vs. Low Temp

Returning to an example from our Superstore data set, suppose management hypothesizes that discounts increase sales. This would imply a positive correlation (As discounts go up so do sales.) However, a business needs more than sales. To be successful a business needs profitable sales!

Let's create a pair of scatter plots to look at discounts, sales and profit. To start, click analysis in the menu-bar, and uncheck "Aggregate Measures." The active worksheet will then override Tableau's default aggregation, and plot each data point. The other worksheets will continue to use the default Tableau behaviors.

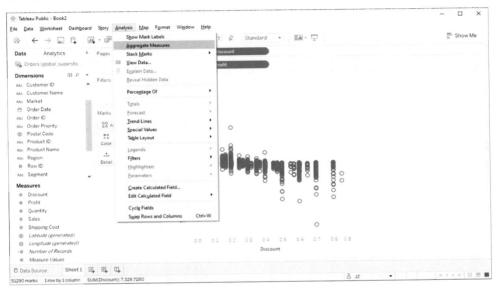

Disaggregated Measures

To investigate the relationship between sales and discounts, we plot the disaggregated sales measure on rows, and the disaggregated discount measure on columns, and Tableau will present dot points, or plots, for each line item in the customer orders.

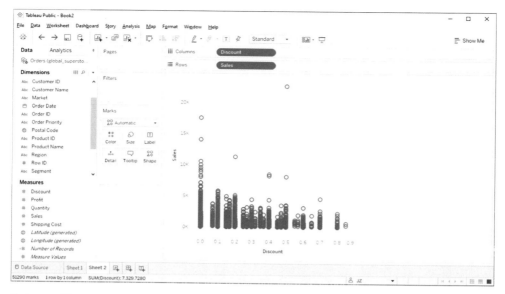

Sales vs. Discount

There looks to be a low, negative correlation, between sales and discounts. The lack of correlation tells us that adding discounts has not correlate to increased sales. Even though we don't have an increase in sales, let's examine profit and discounts.

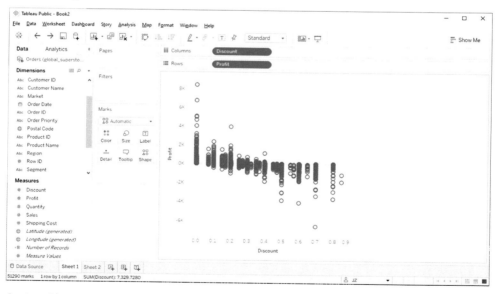

Scatter Plot

The negative sloping direction of the plot indicates inverse correlation between discounts and profit. As discounts increase profit goes down. Although the relationship is not one to one. There are other related factors that might help explain the behavior in the data. For now we can share with management that the initial investigation indicates that discounts do not increase sales. However, this is at a global level. We may find pockets of our data where discounts are more effective. This is the beauty of Tableau. We can start dragging in other dimensions to investigate. Have a go and see what you find.

In addition to the disaggregated scatter plots above, Tableau can also produce scatter plots using aggregated measures. To extend our investigation into profit and discounts, let's create a scatter plot looking at total sales and average discount, by product. Place sales on the rows shelf and discount on the columns shelf. Next, drag the "Product Name" dimension onto detail.

Create Aggregated Scatter Plot

Recall, from the Viz LOD section, that the detail field changes the level of detail. Dragging product name onto the detail field creates a dot for every product name, based on the product's total sales and average discount. Now, we're starting to see something interesting in the data.

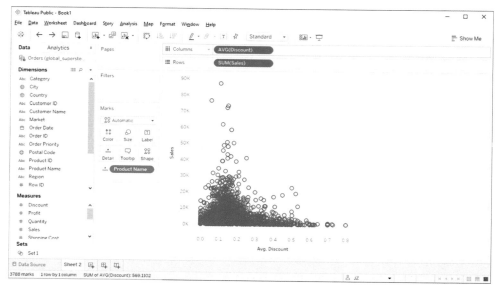

Aggregated Scatter Plot

There appears to be different segments or groups in the discount and product combinations where the discount may drive increased sales. Why might this be?

Looking at the average discount, it is in the normal "Sale" range. For example, a store commonly places products on a 10% discount to drive traffic to the store. It appears for some products that 10% discount increases sales volumes. Over to the right side of the chart, we do not see the same increase in sales, but these discounts are probably less frequent. Perhaps the super high discounts are damaged goods and/or customer service activities. We will revisit this later when we look at using color and size to add even more information to Tableau visualizations.

Create a line chart

Line charts display a series of plots connected with a line to present a continuous progression of data. Line charts illustrate trends in data, and they work well with an ordinal dimension on the horizontal axis. However, time is the most common dimension for line charts, for example, stock prices over a period, inflation rates for the past ten years, or web traffic over a month.

Adding, a date dimension to columns will display the Years across the horizontal axis. Once the data / time is present on the x-axis, dragging a measure to the row shelf automatically creates a line chart in Tableau.

The chart below contains total profit of all the orders for each year, and it is easy to spot that profit is increasing. Note that the year field is green, indicating a continuous date dimension.

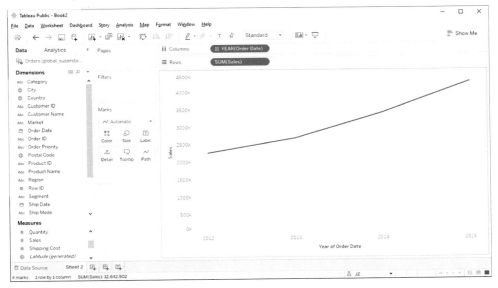

Line Chart

While we can see an increase in sales, there is a lot of hidden detail because we are looking at annual totals. Changing the date to a month-year format typically provides more insight into possible seasonality in sales. Given the cyclical nature of the year, it is quite common for sales to have seasonal highs and lows. Below are the sales aggregated monthly.

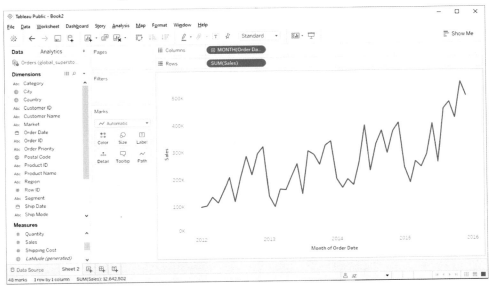

Line Chart - Monthly

Notice the overall upward trend, but the frequent drops throughout the line. That recurring large drop in sales occurs in February, following a December peak. This indicates that something happens early in the calendar years that drives a corresponding reduction in sales. We can investigate the data further, and uncover more of the story. One way to do that might be to combine the line with a bar chart on a dual-axis chart.

Create a dual axis chart

Dual axis charts are a great way to layer information, by including an additional measure on the secondary axis. This is especially useful when the measures use different scales. However dual axis charts require special attention so that the axes are synchronized when possible and do not distort the visual.

Let's walk through an example. Adding profit to the line graph we had in the last section, produces two line graphs. The additional measure also changes the marks card. Notice in the picture below that there are now 3 options in the marks card, "All," "SUM(Sales)," and "SUM(Profit)." Clicking any of these options expands the marks card to adjust the color, size, label, detail, and other options for the selected metric.

Two Measures

1. Make sure SUM(Profit) is selected on the marks card

2. Click the color tile, and select black

3. Click SUM(Sales) in the marks card, and change the mark type to "Bar"

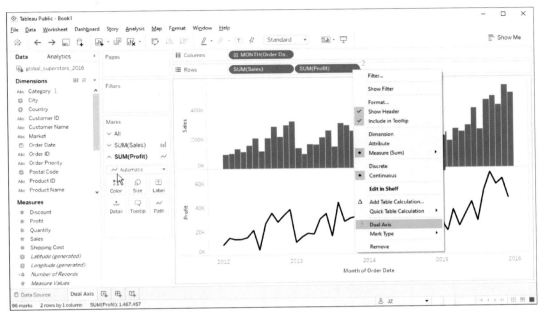

Convert to Dual Axis

1. Click the "Category" dimension, dragging the pill to the color tile in the marks card

2. Right click the "SUM(Profit)" pill in the rows shelf

3. Select Dual Axis from the drop-down menu

Synchronize the Axis

Now we have a stacked bar chart with sales by category, with a profit line graph. All that's left to do is right-click the axis and select "Synchronize Axis."

Initially, the line is a bit distracting, and it doesn't much additional information because it sits atop the bars. This is a common issue with dual axis charts, and something to watch for when reading data visualization. When dual axis charts contain the same unit of measurement, the author should synchronize the scales for both axes. With this sales and profit combination, we know profit should be less than sales because profit equals sales less costs.

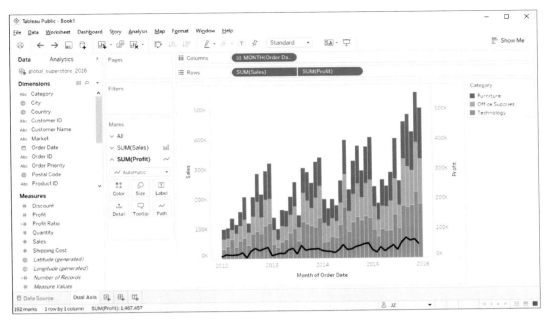

Synchronized Dual Axis Chart

There are a lot of ways to distort information, and it is your responsibility as an analyst to create visuals that accurately portray information. Even with the synchronized axis, we lose some information.

Notice the slope of the profit line in the above and below graphics. We have an appropriate scale for the relationship between profit and sales growth, but the profit line flattens out masking some of the increase. We expect profit to be a smaller nominal amount, and the graph indicates a modest profit margin. However, nominal profit has actually increase almost 5X, from just below 9,000 to 46,000, consistent with the increase in sales from approximately 100,000 to 500,000.

There are a lot of ways to distort information, and it is your responsibility as an analyst to create visuals that accurately portray information. Let's investigate other views of the sales and profit.

The consistent growth in nominal sales and profit indicates that the volumes are increasing, but the overall profitability is relatively flat. While the superstore sells more, the data indicates the superstore may lack the efficiency that typically accompanies the size of a global retailer. Economies of scale should reduce costs with the increased production. To better illustrate this, we can use a profit ratio instead of the profit amount on the secondary axis. (Profit ratio is a calculated field in the data set, and we cover those later in the book.)

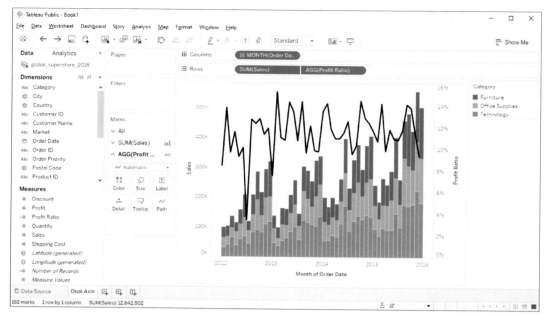

Dual Axis Profit Ratio

Using profit as a percentage of sales, highlights the relatively flat profitability. There is monthly volatility, but overall it bounces around in the 10-15% range. Perhaps, splitting the profit ratio into category would provide more information.

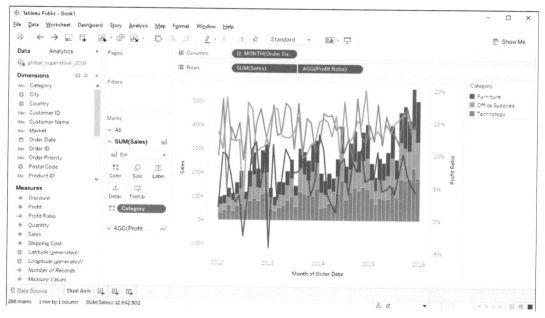

Dual Axis Profit by Category

While the above graph is a bit messy, it aids our data investigation. Later, we cover a coloring trick in a later section tom make it more readable.

Furniture is clearly less profitable than the other two categories, and it is the only category that had negative profits. Now we have something to investigate further. Why is furniture so much less profitable? Is there an opportunity for efficiency gains to increase furniture's profitability, or should the superstore consider exiting furniture sales? These are the types of questions we should expect to discuss with management.

Since profit equals sales minus costs, let's investigate costs using a combined axis chart.

Create a combined axis chart

While dual axis charts are great for showing multiple mark types on the same graph, and comparing volumes to ratios, Tableau also has the ability to produce a combined axis chart. A combined axis chart plots multiple measures on the same axis

There are two ways to create a combined axis chart. First, you can use the "Measure Values" field at the end of the measures list in the data pane. Double-click "Measure Values" or drag the pill into rows. Note that Tableau's default behavior varies based on the method used, and double-clicking automatically adds the measure names to colors.

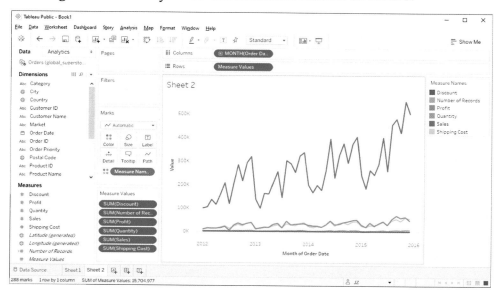

Dragging Measure Values

This pulls all of the measure values onto the same axis, and then we have to remove the measures we don't want. In this example we want to remove the measures that use a scale other than dollar amount. (*This is a good time to call out that removing pills is as simple as dragging them off their card, panel, or shelf. A small red x will appear on the pill, and that tells us Tableau will remove it from the worksheet.*)

Another way to create a combined axis chart is to drop additional measures on the vertical axis. Drag the pill to the axis, hover over the axis, and when two vertical, green bars appear, Tableau will combine measures on the same axis. Let's add Profit and Shipping Cost.

Dragging individual pills to combine

When dragging the individual pills for a combined axis chart, Tableau automatically adds the Measure Names to the filters card and color aesthetic. This makes it easy to identify which field each mark represents, and the filter control let's the user toggle the marks displayed. We will discuss more on filters in the next section.

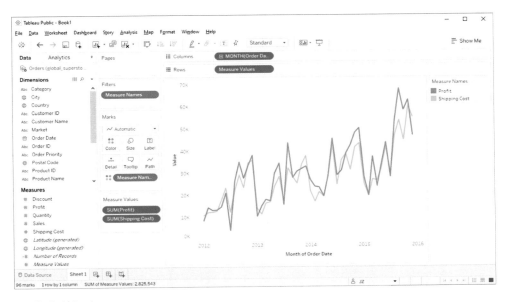

Profit & Shipping

The profit and shipping costs lines are quite close together. Switching them to an area chart, Tableau will stack them on top of each other. However, Tableau still aggregates the measure values independently. Hovering over the line shows you total profit for a month, and if we switch the view to a bar or area chart hovering will show the same value. Since we are trying to decompose sales into profit and costs, we will change the marks from automatic to area.

Profit Shipping Area

Now we see a stacked area chart that shows roughly equal proportions between shipping costs and profit. Unfortunately, the data set only includes the shipping costs, but we can use the sales amount on the secondary axis to imply the amount of other costs. Simply drag sales to the right-hand axis so it appears on the secondary axis. Then, change the mark type to a line, and synchronize the axes. As you make that transition, notice how he entire chart went an odd shade of green. Tableau layers the secondary axis on top of the primary axis, which is why we switch to a line for the mark type.

Profit Shipping Sales

Looking at this graph, we can clearly see the composition of sales as profit (red area), shipping costs (yellow area), and other costs (white space between the red and green). It looks as though any reduction in shipping costs will go straight to profits, we should expect questions from management regarding this topic. If possible, sourcing data for other types of costs will add a lot of value because any reduction in costs will increase profits. Until we have more data costs, the management team can look at reducing shipping cost.

While that is a good use of a combined axis chart, let's explore additional combined axis options to prepare for the exam. First, change the mark type to bar for the Measure Values in the marks card. This gives a similar view to the area chart, but we can place the bars side by side to alter the view.

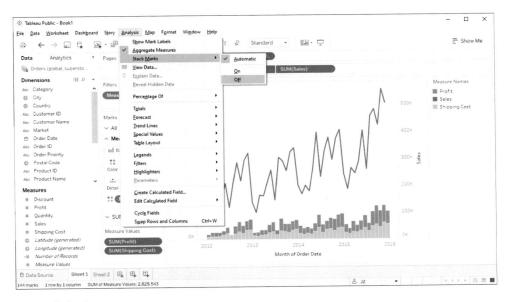

Unstack the bars

Clicking analysis in the menu bar, brings up a menu for stacked. The options are Automatic, On, and Off. Automatic is the default. If we turn off the stacking, Tableau layers the bars on top of each other. With profit and shipping cost amounts so close, we only see a few bits of yellow in the months where shipping costs exceeded profit.

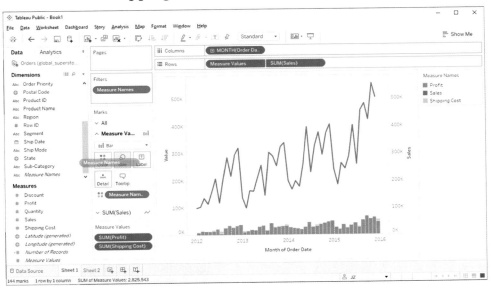

Add Measure Names to Size

However, if we drag the measure names field onto size in the Marks card, Tableau changes the bar sizing to separate / distinguish between the profit and shipping costs bars. Now we have thin red bars that illustrate months where profit exceeded shipping costs. What might make this view more interesting is splitting the sales line into different colors based on the product categories.

Combined Bar Chart Unstacked

This combined, dual-axis chart shows that in some months, the superstore spends more in shipping costs than it earns in profit. Now the question is why? Is a strategic decision based on customer relationship, is there a seasonal pattern, who in the organization might know? These are all questions a good analyst will research using data and talking experts across the business.

Good visualizations raise more questions, and great analysts investigate and analyze a few layers of "Why?" before publishing any analysis. Researching why still involves sharing draft visualizations and soliciting feedback from others, but publishing a public dashboard without covering off a few layers of the simple questions reduces value and insights for the company.

Create a map using geographic data

In the previous examples, our focus was time, but there is another dimension that is critical to understanding the way the world operates, space. Geo-spatial visuals were once extremely complicated to produce, but with the modern data visualization tool set, they are accessible to most data analysts and scientists.

When a data set contains location information, geographic maps provide an opportunity to answer where, as well as why. If the map is not answering that spatial question, it is important for the analyst to challenge why they're using the map in the first place. Spatial questions include things like: which country has the most sales, which countries make up each market, where is the most furniture ordered, where is the most furniture returned?

Just because you can answer those questions with a map doesn't always mean that you should. For example, a horizontal bar graph might fit better in a dashboard to illustrate the country with the most sales. If your can answer the question faster with another visualization, skip the map. Tableau calls out on their website[13], "Maps that answer questions well have both appropriate data representation, and attractive data representation. In other words: the data is not misleading, and the map is appealing."

There are six common map types you can create in Tableau:

- **Proportional Symbol Maps** illustrate quantitative values across specific locations.

- **Choropleth maps (filled maps)** are useful for presenting ratios and aggregate information.

- **Point Distribution Maps** help the viewer identify visual clusters by showing the distribution of data points across locations.

- **Heatmaps (density maps)** show concentrations of points that are overlapping, and are most effective when the data contains many small points in a smaller geographic area.

- **Flow maps (path maps)** connect the movement of something between points over time, for example flight paths.

- **Spider maps (origin-destination maps)** show the start and end points to connect locations, such as transit stations.

Tableau automatically adds a symbol map when you double-click a geographic field, adding it to a blank worksheet. These are useful when visualizing a specific location's quantitative data. From the Global Superstore data, Tableau can use country, zip with postal codes, and city with the cities, and then we can use aggregate measures to add layers to the map.

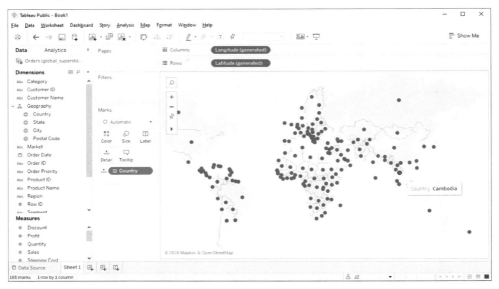

Symbol Map - No Measure

With no measures added to the worksheet, hovering over the dots simply reveals the country name from the detail in the marks card. Double-clicking sales, adds the measure to size in the marks cards, and the country dots change size to reflect the total amount of sales for that country. We can also add the Market field to color in the marks tab, and we the dots will reflect which countries comprise which market.

Symbol Map of Country Sales

Now the viewer can quickly get a sense for which countries are part of which market. While the splits are relatively standard, you can see that Mexico falls under LATAM, and the USCA market only includes the US and Canada. Also, Turkey falls into Asia Pacific. The full granularity available here would take much more space as a table, but if the question is, "What are top 3 countries per market?" then a table might make more sense.

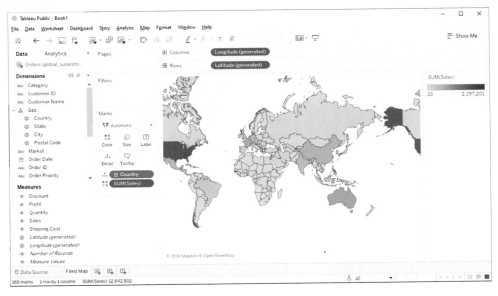

Filled Map of Country Sales

Choropleths (filled map) render shaded polygons based on the geographic detail in the data set. For example, For example, in the map above, Tableau uses the country field to fill in shapes that outline the country borders. To create a filled map, we can click the "Show Me" drop down, and select it from the tiles in the menu. Alternatively, on the marks card, we can click the drop down and select maps.

As mentioned above, just because maps look cool doesn't mean they are the best visualization for the message you need to convey. The filled map takes a lot of space to show such limited information. It's important to always ask, "Why am I using a map here, and how does the map add clarity over other visuals?"

Let's look a heatmap of global sales. Notice that I've changed the mark type to Density, to get the shaded dots. Heatmaps are useful when you have lots of dots on the same point. The darker points represent clusters of activity.

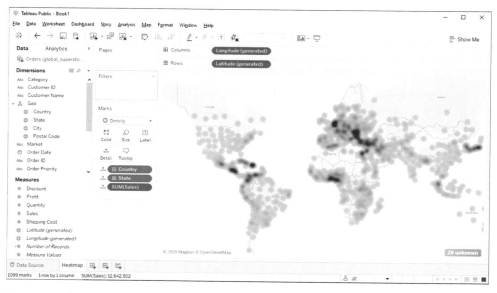

Heatmap of Global Sales

In the heatmap above, we can quickly spot the areas with the most sales, but because we have relatively thin data the heatmap effect requires adjusting the size of the marks and the zoom. This can distort the interpretation of the map. With roughly 51,000 records in our data set, we don't have a high enough concentration of volumes to warrant the heatmap. It is better to use heatmaps when we have large volumes of data in a smaller geographic area. For example, the heatmap below shows Yellow Taxi pickups in New York City in January 2019. There are millions of records in that data set, and a New Yorker will quickly spot Manhattan as one of the most popular pickup locations.

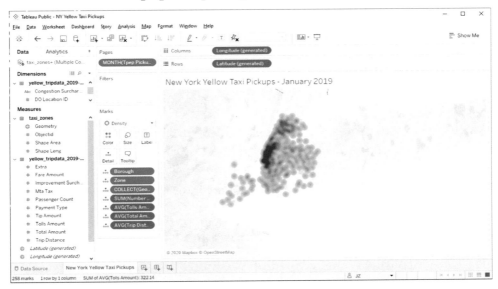

Yellow Taxi Heatmap

Similarly, point distribution maps also benefit from higher volumes of data. Take, for example, this map of Tornadoes in the US from 1950 to 2018.

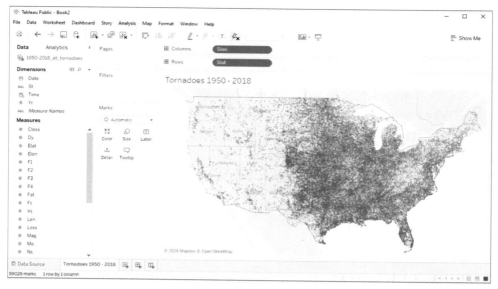

Tornado Point Distribution

The geographic data for this map is contains the exact latitude and longitude where each tornado started, and the volume of points produces a similar result to the heatmap, but without masking the quantity. It looks like more tornadoes than taxi pickups, but there are far more taxi pickups.

One last time, maps require thought and purpose. Don't use a map because the map is appealing. Make sure the map is informative.

For a deep dive into maps, check out the Tableau Maps Solutions page[14] and the Maps and Geographic Data Analysis Tableau help page[15].

Create a chart to show specific values (cross-tab, highlight table)

Extending the idea that visualizations need to do more than look pretty, sometimes a good old-fashioned table is the best way to convey information. Tableau refers to tables as crosstabs.

When double-clicking a measure, Tableau adds it to the rows shelf, and creates a graphic, by default. However, if we start with dimensions, like category and sub-category, Tableau creates a crosstab. You can drag your measure into the desired location on the table, or you can drag it to the text button on the Marks Card. Alternatively, once the mark type is text, you can double click the field.

Crosstab

Now if we double-click a measure, like Sales, Tableau adds it by default to Text in the Marks Card. This creates a table with the total sales by category and sub-category.

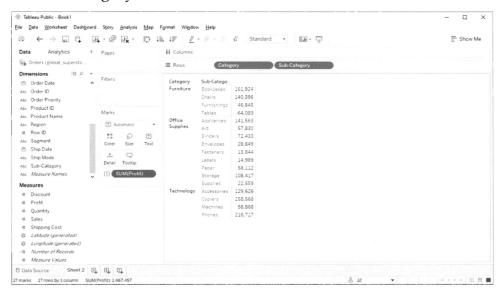

Sales Crosstab

If you've used pivot tables in Excel, you will find this layout familiar. If we add market to the columns shelf, Tableau will expand the table to include a volume for total sales in each market. Additionally, there is a Totals menu in the analysis drop-down from the menu bar. It contains selections to include row and column totals, subtotals, and totals to the table.

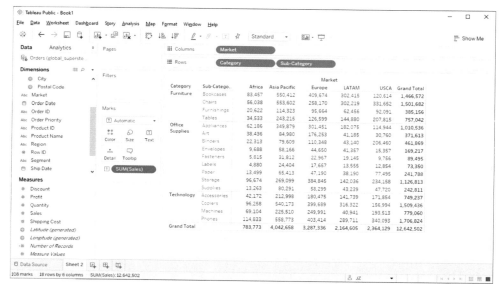

Crosstab with Totals

This crosstab is a good way to see sales but converting it to a highlight table may make it quicker to scan. We can make the switch by dragging sales onto color in the Marks Card instead of the Label.

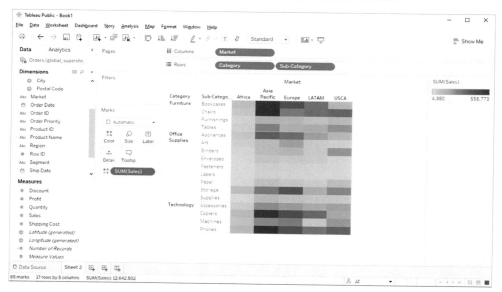

Highlight Table

Now we can quickly see the breakdown of sales volumes by category and market, with the dark blue highlighting the highest sales areas. IF we want to see the actual sales amounts in each cell, we simply need to display the labels. clicking the label button in the Marks Card, brings up the label options, and all we need to do is check the box for show labels.

Highlight Table with Labels

Now it is easy to see the total sales amount, along with the highest volume categories and markets. And with that, you are able to create all of the basic charts required for the Tableau Desktop Specialist exam!

Organize data and apply filters

The velocity at which humans and machines create data is astonishing. By 2025, there are predictions that global storage will be around 163 zettabytes of data. If you took 1 terabyte hard drives out of the average laptop (2.5in), that data would stretch to Mars and back![16]

With all that information, organizing and filtering the data we use is essential to driving meaningful outcomes. We can create pretty visuals in Tableau, but the real power lies in how easily we can interrogate the data to drive insights.

It's worth repeating that a good analyst is constantly asking why. A good visual prompts these questions, and a good visualization tool allows user to investigate questions on the spot.

Here's a typical line of questioning:

1. "Why are sales up? Let me use Tableau to filter by location to see if geography drives the increase."

2. "Hmm, let's look at categories, and subcategories."

3. "Now, what about the overlay between geography and categories, or perhaps even specific products?"

Questions are good, and a seasoned analyst has built up a strong why muscle from asking lots of questions. With Tableau and the wealth of free data on the web, it is easy to start your training. You've learned how to connect to data, clean it up a bit, and create standard data visualizations. Now it's time to learn techniques to probe the data for hidden patterns.

Tableau has three primary methods to organize and filter your data:

1. Filter - a dimension (occasionally a measure) that sifts through the data set for specific records based on the field's values

2. Group - creates categories using multiple values within a dimension

3. Set - a subset of the data matching criteria based on existing dimension in the data set

Add a filter to the view

Filtering is a great way to drill down into the data to answer the questions that the initial view of the data presents. Filters apply to the current worksheet by default. However, it is possible to apply a filter to multiple, or even all, sheets that use the same data source.

Filters are intuitive, and that makes them more user-friendly when publishing a dashboard or report for public consumption. The report's consumers don't need to be Tableau experts to quickly infer how to use the filters. Filters apply to the current sheet by default, but it is possible to adjust the filter settings to apply to several, or even all, worksheets.

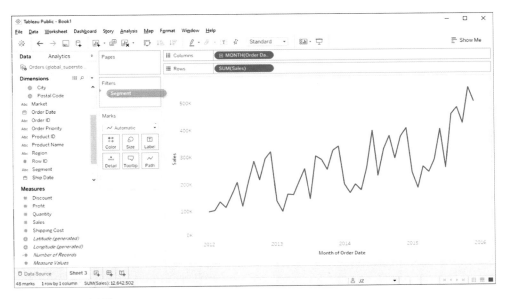

Drag pill to add filter

It is possible to add filters to visualizations by dragging fields to the filters shelf and by right-clicking fields to select "Filter" or "Show Filter." Adding the filter typically brings up the filter settings dialogue box.

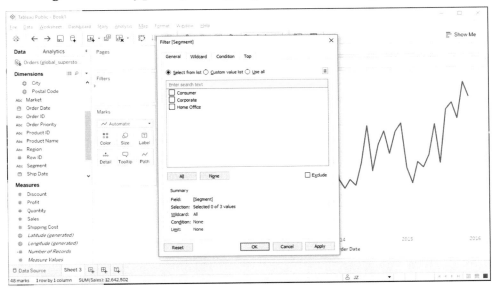

Filter Settings Pop-up

There are four tabs in the filters setting box, General, Wildcard, Condition, and Top. General is straight forward; what you select is included, unless you check the exclude box. Then your selections are excluded. Wildcard filtering allows a user to filter on partial string matching. Condition filtering applies conditional filters based on field values or formulas, and the top tab allows the user to filter for the "Top N" values by field or formula.

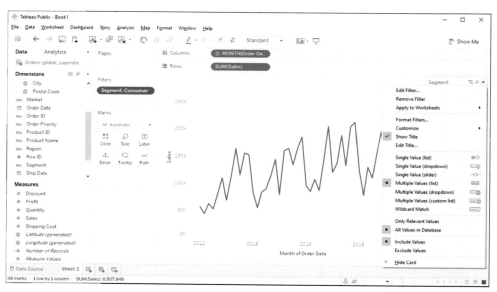

Filter control Layout

Right-clicking the field in the filter shelf, or anywhere else for that matter, provides an option to "Show Filter." Clicking "Show Filter" adds a filter control card to the right-hand side of the visual. There are many options for how the control displays, and these vary based on data and filter types. Click the small triangle drop-down menu on the filter control, and the filter menu lists the available options.

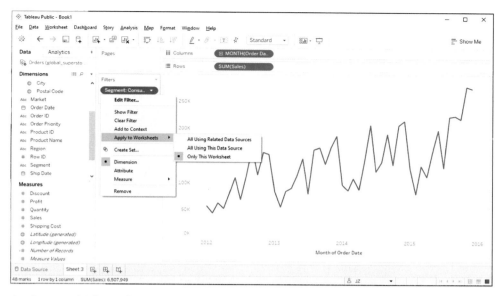

Apply to multiple worksheets

Another feature available from the right-click, drop-down menu, is "Apply to Worksheets." When adding a filter to a worksheet, Tableau's default action only applies a filter to the active worksheet. This "Apply to Worksheets" setting overrides the default, allowing the filter to apply to all, or a selection, of the worksheets using the data source.

The Wildcard, Condition, and Top dynamic filtering options are extremely powerful, and returning to our maps discussion, remember to consider why you're using them. Are they informative, or is it just cool to have the interactive visual? It needs to be informative above all else.

Add a context filter

Context filters perform like view filters, but Tableau processes them earlier in sequence of queries it runs to generate the view. When a context filter is set, Tableau uses the context filter first, restricting the data used in the remainder of the view calculations.

Standard view filters use only the subset of data in the context filter results. This improves performance because Tableau is working with less data, and context filters are an efficient way to create dependent numerical or top N filters, like the top 10 customers within a state. As an example, let's apply two standard filters, one that filters the state of Texas and one that filters the top 10 customers by sales. Tableau calculates the top N customers using the whole data set, and Tableau filters by state. What do you notice about our list of the top 10 customers in Texas by sales?

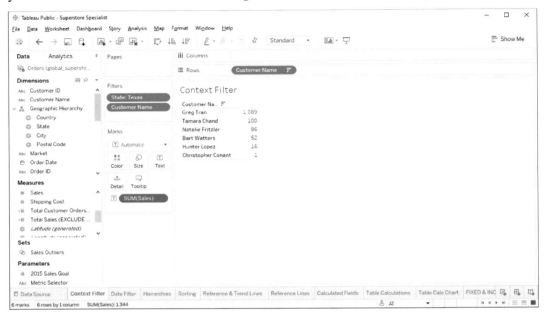

Standard view filters

There are only six customers in the list. There are more than 6 customers in Texas, but they don't appear in the view because Tableau runs the two queries to filter by state and to filter by the top 10 customers. These queries run in parallel, so the top 10 customers globally are matched with the list of customers who ordered something in Texas. Evidently only 6 of the top 10 customers globally ordered items in Texas.

To ensure our list contains the top 10 customers in Texas, we change the state filter to a context filter. Right-click the filter pill for state, and select "Add to Context." The pill changes from blue to gray, indicating it is part of the context. Now, Tableau creates a list of customers in Texas, and then runs the top N calculation.

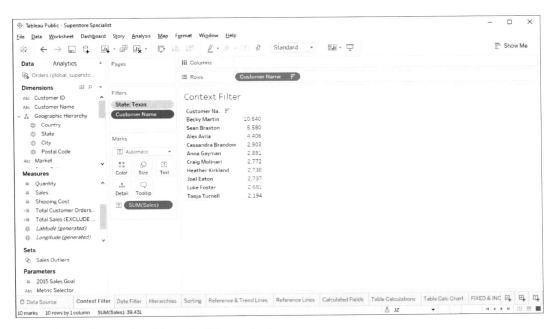

Grey Filter Indicates that it's part of the context

Now, there are 10 customers in our list, and none of them were on the first list of 6 customers. Applying the state and top N customers filters, as standard dimension filters produced a list of the Texas sales for the top 10 global customers. Notice the highest sales amount in the initial list of customers is half the amount of sales for the 10th person on our new list.

Setting the context is important to ensure that Tableau produces output that is consistent with your question. With the context filter, we answer, "Who are the top 10 customers in Texas by sales?" With the two standard dimension filters, we answer the question, "Who are our top 10 customers by sales, and how much did they order in Texas?"

Not only does the context filter provide the answer to the question the manger asked, it also improves the query performance because the context filter runs first. this reduces the number of records used in all subsequent filter queries and calculations. In our example, Tableau only needs to use the 985 records from Texas, instead of all 51,290 from the full data set.

In a large corporate setting, the analysis tends to use "data at scale," which refers to the big data generated by large business. When analyzing billions or even millions of records, that reduction in records used makes a huge performance impact.

Add a date filter

Date filters vary with the use of discrete and continuous dates. The discrete date filters present themselves the same as the other dimension filters, and the continuous date filters provide different options for date ranges, relative dates, and start/end dates. allow the user to restrict the data in the visualization based on date fields. The date filters can apply to relative dates, a range of dates, or specific values within the parts (years, quarters, months, etc.) of a date field.

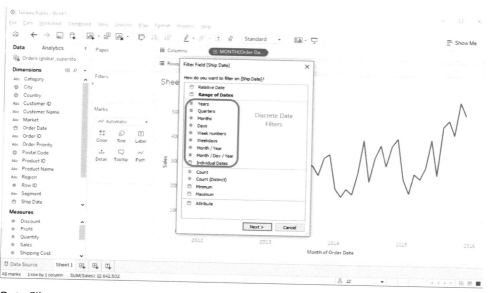

Date Filter menu

Dragging a date field to the filters shelf, brings up the above menu. There are a mix of options are for discrete and continuous dates, and the first two are the most common continuous date filters.

"Range of Dates" allows the user to set a start date, an end date, or both, and then Tableau will refresh the view with all date from after, before, or between the selected date range. The filter menu, let's the user specify starting ranges, and then the filter control allows users to adjust the date range, when viewing the visualization.

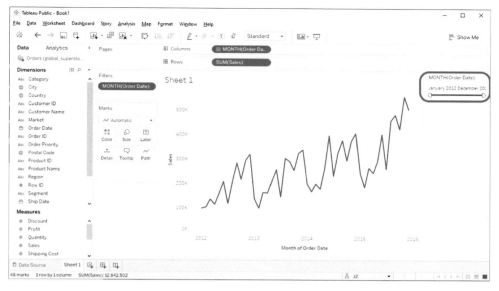

Date Range Filter

Tableau presents the user a slider filter control. The slider has 1 or 2 slide points depending on whether or not the with sliders on one or both ends of a line for the start and end dates of the range. When the filter is a start date or end date only filter, the line only slides from the open-ended value.

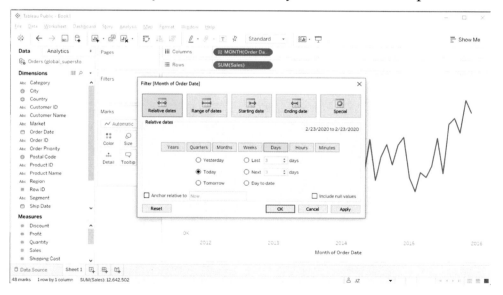

Continuous Date Filter Settings

"Relative Date" brings up the menu for selection options that leverage the current date. The relative dates base themselves off today's date by default, but there is an option to set an anchor date. Tableau then calculates the date range using the date part selected, year, month, day, or any other. For example, on a sales dashboard, it might be useful at the store level to have it show a rolling 13 months, and at the salesperson level, it might make since to line it up with commissions payments intervals, say quarterly.

Often, the relative dates are referred to as rolling periods. Typically, it makes sense to use a rolling 13 months, 9 quarters, and 8 days. Those intervals give the viewer a comparison value. Commonly there are patterns in data that align with dates. In a monthly report, being able to compare this year's January numbers to last January helps the viewer adjust for seasonality, or cyclical patterns.

The filter control looks similar to the settings box, and lets the user adjust the intervals on the fly.

Filter Control for Relative Date

Grouping Data

Grouping data uses dimension members to create a higher-level category. When created, visual groups highlight the members separately, and label groups combine the members in the view.

When groups are relatively static through time, they will likely have fields in the data source already. For example, the Superstore data includes category and subcategory fields that group products. There are 3 categories, 17 subcategories, and 3,788 products. Depending on the objective of our investigation, we can use the category or subcategory fields to group the information. It is less likely we will need to see detail on all 3,788 products.

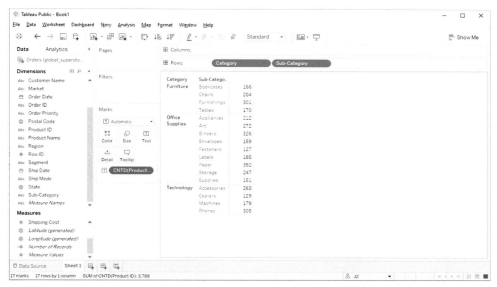

Categories

Sometimes the source data does note contain these groupings. Perhaps, the groups change, and it is easier to adjust the reporting than the database, or perhaps the marketing team wants to trial some new groupings to improve the store layouts. Regardless, Tableau can quickly create groups on the fly.

For example, the 9 Office Supplies sub-categories are quite diverse, and we may want to group related sub-categories to reduce the number of members in the sub-category dimension. For example, Envelopes, Paper, and Labels, could combine to become "Stationery," and Binders, Storage, and Fasteners make sense as "Organization."

We can create this grouping three ways:

1. Visual Group - select multiple marks in the visualization

2. Labels Group - select multiple labels in the visualization

3. Create Group Menu - right-click the field in the data pane, and select the group option under create

Creating a visual group

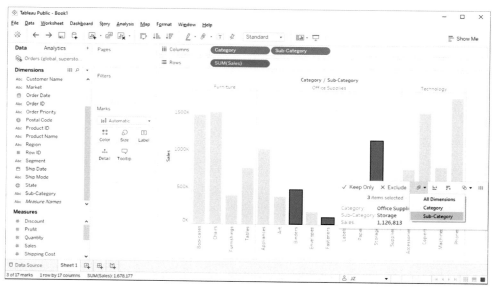

Create Visual Group

Highlight the marks that you want to group together, and let the mouse cursor hover over a highlighted mark. (Hold the Control (Ctrl) key on Windows or the Command key on a Mac to click and select multiple marks.)

Next, click the group icon in the tool tip menu that pops up. In the tool tip menu that pops up, the paper-clip icon is the group button.

Alternatively, right-clicking a highlighted mark, produces a drop-down menu, with an option for Group.

Either way, selecting "All Dimensions" adds a group to the dimensions in the data pane across Category and Subcategory.

All Dimensions Visual Group

Notice new dimension labelled "Category & Subcategory (Group),"
highlighted in the data data pane. Tableau creates a new group dimension,
and adds it to color by default. Also, the value in the legend displays the
group name, including both the Category and Sub-Category field values,
and the legend contains the unselected marks grouped as "Other."

Selecting the Category visual group, creates a new dimension, "Category
(Group)," and the "Category (Group)" includes all members of the Office
Supplies category. The legend contains "Office Supplies" and "Other."

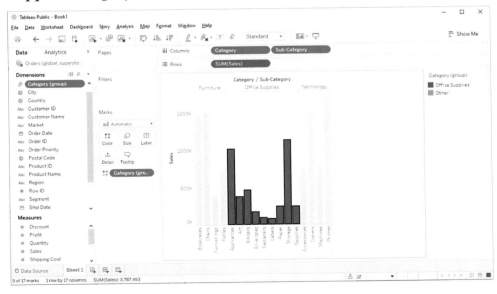

Category Visual Group

Finally, selecting Sub-Category creates the "Sub-Category (group)" dimension, and now the legend contains the three sub-categories we selected.

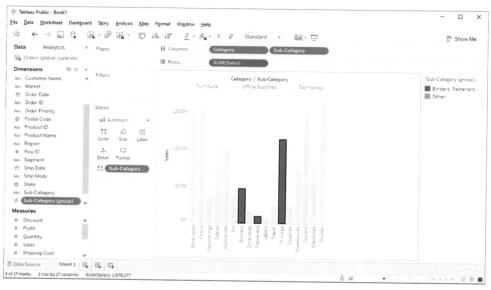

Sub-Category Visual Group

By default, visual groups will present as the color, and will broadly create two groups, selected dimension members and other. When you refresh your data set, and new dimension members will automatically go into the "other" group.

Create a group using labels

Using the labels to create a group combines the members into a single dimension member, and by default, Tableau replaces the existing view dimension.

Holding down the control (Windows) or command (Mac) key while selecting axis labels selects multiple values. The selection below are three subcategories that are office supplies related to organizing the office.

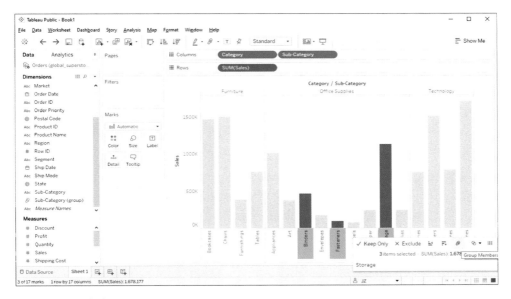

Creating a Label Group

Once selected, we can right-click on one of them to create a group, or click the group icon in the tool tip buttons. Tableau's default action is to create a new dimension with Sub-Category, grouping these values together. Then it automatically uses the new dimension to replace Sub-Category on the columns shelf.

Label Group

Now, the view contains a Sub-Category of "Binders, Fasteners, Storage," and it has the second highest value on the chart. Grouping can reveal different, hidden patterns in the data, and is a great way to align the original design of a system with the current reality of the business.

Perhaps, our new superstore layout includes these items in an "Organizing" section of the shop, but the IT update to reflect that in source system data is months away.

Maybe, we through our analysis we realized customers are buying these items together, and we want to highlight a potential cross-selling opportunity, by putting these items together. If they were together, would more customers by all three?

Before we move on to sets, let's look edit group dialogue box and its differences for visual and label groups. As previously mentioned, the visual group has two groups, "Other" and the one we created. Conversely, the labels group has the group we created along with the remaining members of the dimension.

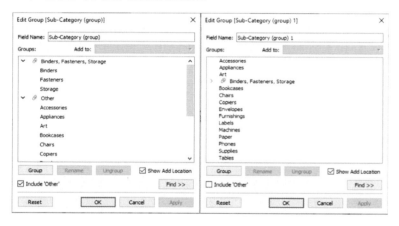

Grouping Data Summary

As a final note on groups, it is important to understand how they respond to changes in the underlying data. Visual groups create a group labeled "Other", and if a new value appears in the underlying data, the "Other" group automatically includes the new value. In our example, we created a static group of "Organisation" items. If the Superstore added a new organization Sub-Category, like "Folders," Tableau by default includes it in the "Other" group. We need to edit the group settings to include "Folder" under "Organisation."

With label groups, the new Sub-category needs to be added to the group, as well. However, it will still show up as a dimension member because label groups do not create an "Other" group.

Both visual and label groups are effective tools to simplify visualizations when dimensions contain a large number of members. With the label groups, we can even create additional levels in hierarchies.

Here is a link to the Tableau site[17] for more detail on creating groups, and the next section covers the detail on creating and using sets, which conversely to groups, have the ability to respond even more dynamically to changes in the underlying data.

Create a set

From the Tableau website[18], "Sets are custom fields that define a subset of data based on some conditions." The set fields are useful when comparing and interrogating subsets of your data.

There are two types of sets, fixed and dynamic. *Fixed sets* contain a static subset of values or data points; whereas, *dynamic sets* update based on formula results and changes in the underlying data.

The way Tableau presents sets is using the "In/Out" logic. A dynamic set of the top 3 salespeople by total sales, will show the performance of the top 3 salespeople (In) compared to everyone else (Out). This will highlight the difference between the top sellers and everyone else, allowing leaders to dig for clues as to what might improve sales performance.

Fixed sets are a powerful tool for digging deeper, and they become even more powerful when used with groups and other Tableau features. Commonly, fixed sets may be used in assessing performance of different treatment groups or segments.

This process is commonly referred to as A/B testing and based on the statistical methods for significance testing. For example, marketing may decide to randomly show half of the company's website user version A of a page, and the other half version B. Then, you can test for whether page A or page B drives more sales. Additionally, you can leverage sets to look at the performance of pages A and B across a range of additional dimensions such as age, gender, and other demographics.

For our practical example, we will use a fixed set to explore the sales and discount relationship.

To create a fixed set, select marks in the visualization and click the set icon in the tool tip. Alternatively, right-clicking a dimension in the data pane, there is an option to create a set in the drop down menu. The editing interface differs for each of those methods, and the behaviors differ between the fixed and dynamic sets. Using the marks to create a set, results in a "fixed set." This means that the set will include a constant subset of the data to present as IN the set.

Let's return to our scatter plot of total sales against discount, with product name on detail.

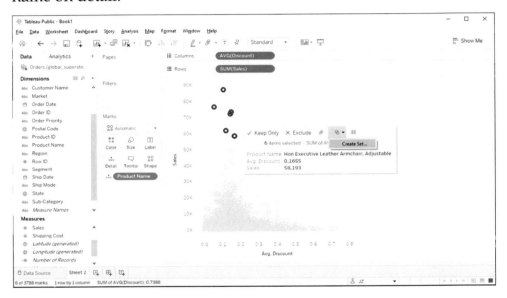

Selecting Marks to Create a Set

Create the set, by selecting multiple marks in the visualization, and then hover over, or right-click one of the marks. Next, click the set icon in the tool tip, as in the example image above. Tableau responds with a "Create Set" dialogue box.

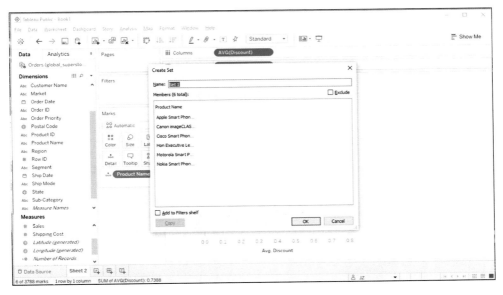

Create Set from Marks

Let's name the set "High sales, lower average discount," click "OK," and then add it to color on the marks card.

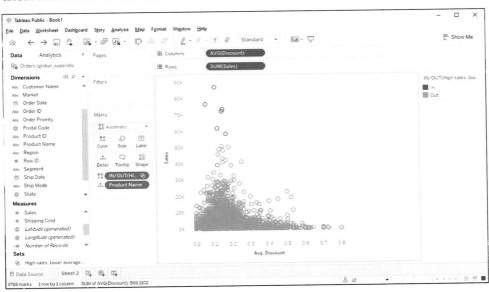

Coloring with set

Now, the visual calls attention to the plots for products in the set compared to out of the set, but we can do that with highlighting. The power with the set is that we can layer it into the viz LOD. If we drag segment to "Detail" on the marks card, we can see the specific plots from the set compared to the rest of plots at the product and segments level of detail.

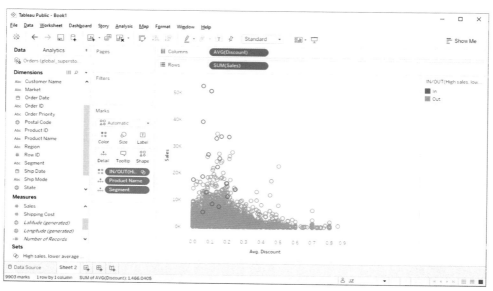

Layering with sets

Adding the segment detail altered the shape of the scatter plot, and calls out some additional insights. Here we can see that the response, or use of discounts, varies across customer segments. The same product has different total sales, based on whether the customer was in the consumer, home office, or corporate segment.

To investigate further on your own, select one of the blue dots, and create a group on segment. Then look into the average discount and total sales for the product in each segment. What do you notice? Is there a segment that appears to be more or less responsive to discounts?

There are a few additional set features in Tableau that you should know at a very high level. Below is a screen-grab from the Tableau site's[19] section on icons and visual cues. It defines icons associated with the 4 ways sets are created.

⊘	The field is a user-defined set. See Create Sets ⬚.
⬚	The field is a server named set.
⬚	The field is a set that was automatically created as a result of an action.
⬚	The field is a user filter, used when publishing to the web. See Restrict Access at the Data Row Level.

Set Icons

We created user sets, and we will touch on actions in a later section. Knowing that the server named sets and the user filters exist is sufficient for the scope of the Specialist exam.

Why use sets over filters

A common question from visualization analysts is, "why go through that trouble with the sets, when I can just use filters?"

Sets become a field that is easy to reuse throughout a workbook, and when sets are updated, the update flows through the entire workbook. By contrast, filters apply only to specified sheets, and by default only to the initial sheet using the filter. Additionally, if you have a cross-section of multiple dimensions that you uncover while filtering, creating a set makes it easier to use that cross-section in the visualizations.

Sets also become part of the metadata and Stored Data Source (.tds file), making sets easier to share across workbooks.

Those are strong cases for sets, and you need to know them for the test. However, in the office, report users may require training to get the most out of sets. Conversely, they are likely familiar with the concept of filtering from Excel because most professionals have some exposure to the ubiquitous spreadsheet software. Ultimately the determining factor will be performance, the task at hand, and even a bit of personal/user preference.

Organize dimensions into a hierarchy

Tableau has the capability to process data using a hierarchical data structure. This allows for the nesting of fields and values in a specific order. For example, Product, Category, and Sub-category are all related. The product sits in a sub-category, which is part of a category.

Some hierarchies are created by default when Tableau connects to a data source, for example the decomposition of date parts. When you add a date it defaults to year, and when you click the plus symbol in that date pill, the field expands with a second pill for the next date part, quarter. Clicking the plus symbol in the quarter pill expands to add a month pill, and this continues through the date parts.

Date Hierarchies

In addition to the automatic hierarchies, we can create custom hierarchies. Tableau also includes the functionality to create custom hierarchies. In the Superstore data set, there are several dimensions related to product, and perhaps the user wants the ability to easily drill down from category to product name. We can right-click category in the data pane and select create hierarchy.

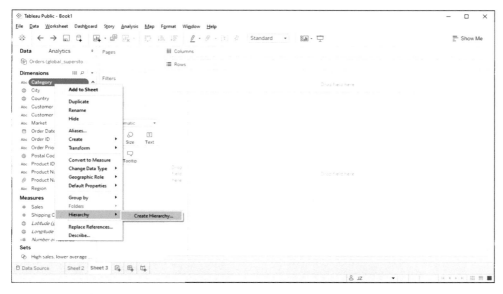

Create Hierarchy

This pops up an input box to name the hierarchy, and we will call this one "Product Hierarchy." Conversely, you can drag pills in the data pane to create hierarchies, and then click to rename the hierarchy in the data pane.

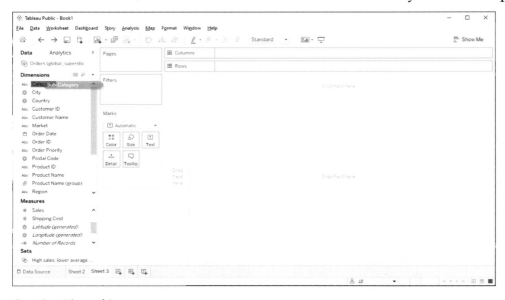

Creating Hierarchies

Once the hierarchy is in the data pane, we can continue adding pills to the hierarchy. Notice below, that I added the Category, Sub-Category, and Product Name fields to Product Hierarchy. Now, adding the hierarchy itself, or any of the fields in the hierarchy, will include that plus symbol to drill into the hierarchy. We can also drag the dimensions around in the hierarchy to put them in order from the top level (Category) to the lowest level (Product Name).

Geographic Hierarchy

This is a useful tool for dimensions where the underlying data maintains a hierarchical relationship.

You now have the essential tools to organize and filter your data as a Tableau Desktop Specialist. Let's move on to applying analytics!

Apply analytics to a worksheet

Analytics are available through the analytics pane, analytics drop-down in the menu bar, and in the view itself. The "Analysis" menu in the menu bar contains totals, trend lines, and the analytics pane contains summary, modelling, and custom analytics. Within the view itself, right-clicking, hovering, and some editing dialog boxes will contain options to layer in analysis.

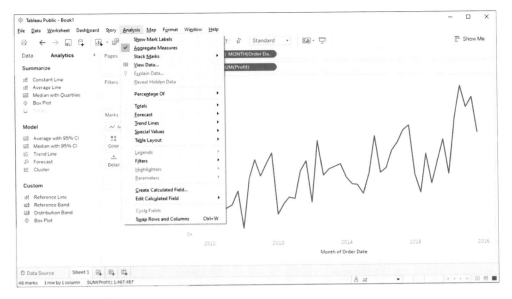

Analytics in the Worksheet

Analytics are useful tools to convey scope, scale, and descriptive statistics. Used effectively the various analytics enhance the business context of the information contained in the visualizations we create. This in turn facilitates the robust, informed discussion required to drive meaningful outcomes from dashboards and reports. A simple and effective piece of analytics is the ability to sort the data.

Add a manual or a computed sort

Sorting data is useful tool for ranking data, based on either its values or the values of another field in the data set. Tableau has the ability to apply both manual and computed sorts. Using a computed sort , Tableau will organize a dimension alphabetically in ascending or descending order, based on the alphabetical order of the characters. For the Ship Mode field in the Superstore data set, an ascending sort is First Class, Same Day, Second Class, and then Standard Class. However, you may want to arrange Ship Modes in a more hierarchical order, such as Standard Class, Second Class, First Class, and then Same Day. This is possible with a manual sort.

Tableau makes it incredibly simple to apply sorts from almost anywhere in the worksheet, and if you remember from the section on how to manage data properties, it is possible to set a default sort by right-clicking a dimension in the data pane. The default sort options are limited to data source order, alphabetic, field, and manual. As in the example below, right-clicking a bill in the view to apply a sort produces the full range of sort options, which also includes nested sorting.

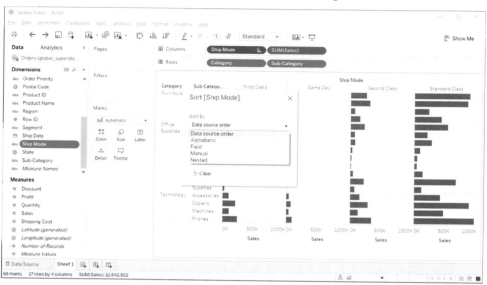

Sort from Pill

A nested sort considers the panes independently, sorting the rows within the pane, whereas a non-nested sort considers the values across all panes. The non-nested view sorts the same order of values in every pane. Take for example this view of market sales by category. There is computed field sort on category by sum of sales. Notice how every market shows the categories in the same order, office supplies, furniture, and then technology.

Comparative sort (non-nested)

Now compare that to this nested sort on category by sum of sales, and notice the difference. The order of category changes within the pane for each market. Furniture is the top category by sales in every market except for Asia Pacific and LATAM.

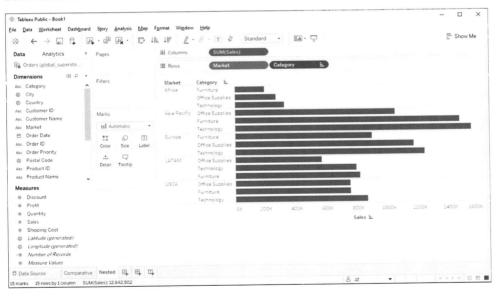

Nested Sort

This is a very powerful feature that requires careful attention because it can easily distort the interpretations of the view. In some cases, you may want to disable sorting so that viewers don't inadvertently alter the message. This can be done from the Worksheet drop-down menu on the menu bar, using the "Show Sort Controls" option. This removes the ability to sort the visualization itself from the axis or the headers.

That's right, Tableau includes sort controls in the axis and headers of the view itself. Below is the icon that appears when you hover the mouse over the header.

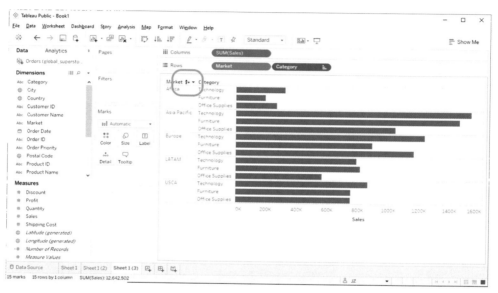

Sort from Header

Notice the small A-Z icon that appears. This will sort the Market dimension alphabetically, experiment with left and right clicking to get a feel for the controls available through the header.

Additionally, you can sort the view using the axis. Sorting on the axis adds computed sorts based on the values in the view. Pictured below are the small sort icons that appear when hovering. Whereas the A-Z icon indicates alphabetical sorting. The bars indicate sorting based on values.

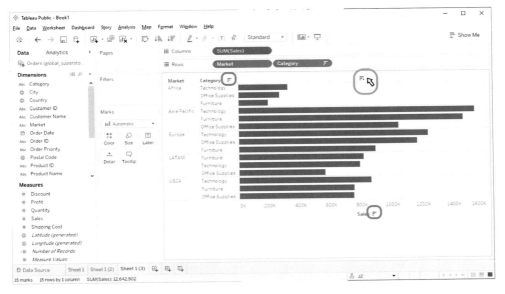

Sort from Axis

The sort icons highlighted in blue indicate that the field is part of the existing sorts. The sort icon in orange includes a small down arrow that indicates clicking it will apply a descending sort to the value on that axis, and it only appears when the mouse cursor hovers over the axis. The sort icon next to the Sales label would change to include the arrow if we move the mouse to hover over it.

Finally, there are two buttons next to each other in the toolbar that apply a sort in either ascending or descending order. These will change the existing sort to either ascending or descending order, and if there is no sorting in the view, they apply the default sorts for the fields in the view.

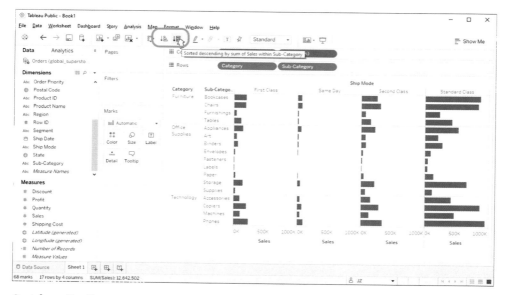

Sort from Toolbar

For further information on advanced sorting options, check out the Tableau site[20].

Add a reference line or trend line

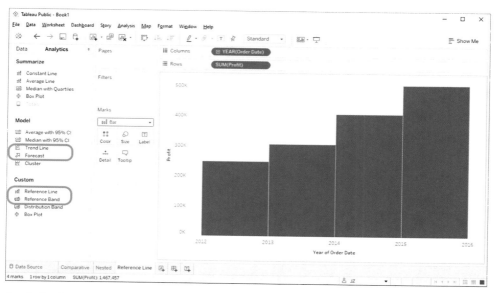

Analytics Pane

Reference lines and trend lines provide scale and scope to highlight patterns and directional movement in data, and Tableau calculates them at the table, pane, or cell level. Trend lines are also available in the Analysis drop-down on the menu bar, and both Trend and Reference lines are available in analytics tab within the data pane (pictured above). However, there must be data in the worksheet to add analytics, and trend lines require the data to contain a date field. If the options are grayed out, then Tableau needs additional or different fields to make the calculations.

Once the visualization has data, drag the reference line from the analytics pane into the image. Notice the pop-up over the view with buttons for Table, Pane, and Cell. Dropping the pill on one of these buttons applies the reference line at that level of granularity. Otherwise, Tableau adds the line at the Pane level by default.

Drag & Drop Reference Line

As mentioned, Tableau adds the reference line to the entire table, each pane, or even each cell of information, and both constant value and computed reference lines are available. The options for computed reference lines are Total, Sum, Min, Max, Average, and Median. Furthermore, Tableau can create reference lines, bands, distributions, and box plots.

Once you drop the reference line pill on the view, Tableau brings up the "Edit Reference Line, Band, or Box" dialog menu. Here you can set the reference type, context (table, pane, cell), and other attributes. The default line uses the average value of the profit sums, but clicking the drop-down let's you change the calculation. In the example below, we set a constant value.

Constant values provide useful context for the views. We have the sales numbers, but on their own, the numbers don't tell us whether they're good or bad. If sales are $2.25M and costs are twice that, the company is in trouble. Depending on the audience, it may not be appropriate to include the cost details, or it may simply be more motivational to show a sales goal instead of costs.

Reference Line Settings

In the image above, the label is set to "2012 Target," and the value is set 1,500,000. This makes it easy to see 2012 sales performance against the 2012 target, and it is possible to add additional reference lines for the other years. To assist with interpretation, let's make the line green to easily mark that the team met the sales target. This can be done int he bottom of the edit dialog box. Additionally, you can bring up additional formatting options using the format menu bar drop-down , or right-clicking the reference line.

The view below includes multiple reference lines representing annual sales targets. Suppose the management team needs to set the 2016 goal. Here we can see that after missing the 2014 goal, the 2015 increase was not as large. Now that sales back on track, what should the 2016 target be?

Using a trend line, you can indicate the upward direction of sales growth, and the management team can use the trend to help set the 2016 target. Dragging the Trend Line pill from the model section of the analytics pane adds a trend line to the

Dragging a Trend Line

Notice that there are a few options. Tableau runs statistical regression analysis to calculate the trend line, and there are 5 regression types available. Different data patterns and shapes indicate the optimal regression method, but that is out of scope for this text. I recommend a quick search of the web for some light reading or videos on the subject. The sales trend here in the Superstore data set presents a linear trend, which is the default.

Now we can see the upward trend of the data to get a feel for a more realistic target. Hovering over the trend line, we can also see the regression formula generated by Tableau.

Trend Line

Notice that 2013 and 2014 were below the trend line, and 2015 finished slightly above. This indicates that we may want to keep the sales target increase consistent with the jump from 2014 from 2015. Without a significant change in sales tactics, markets, or customer behavior, it is unlikely the trend will change. This indicates a lower likelihood of sales increasing by more than $1M.

An important item to note here is how the view presentation will distort the trends. Typically, a trend should be presented in a landscape orientation, meaning the graph is wider than it is tall. Switching the date dimension to it's continuous value changes the aspect ratio and the perceived slope of the trend.

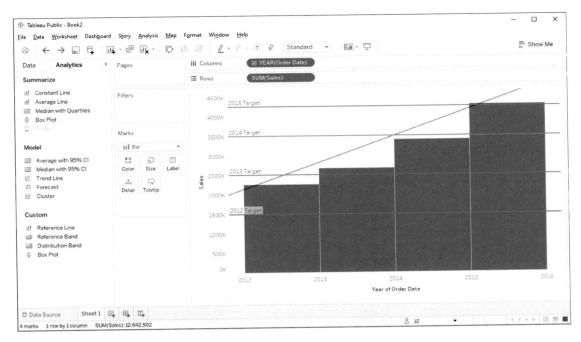

Trend Line Continuous Date

Hovering over the trend line displays the regression formula in the tool tip, and right-clicking brings up a drop-down menu, with an "Edit Trend Line" option. This pops up a dialogue box to edit the trend line's settings.

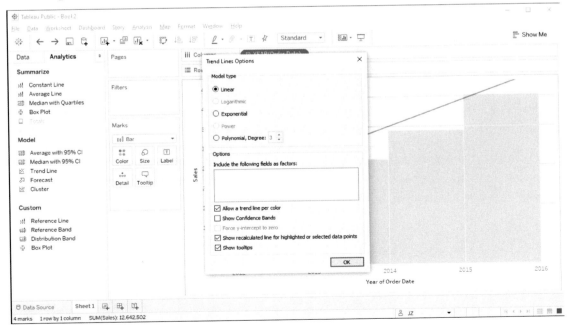

Trend Line Settings

There are also two options when right-clicking the trend line to "Describe Trend Line" and "Describe Trend Model." These will give you detail on the regression equation. Describing the trend line provides the slightly more detail than hovering over the trend line, and describing the trend model provides expanded model details.

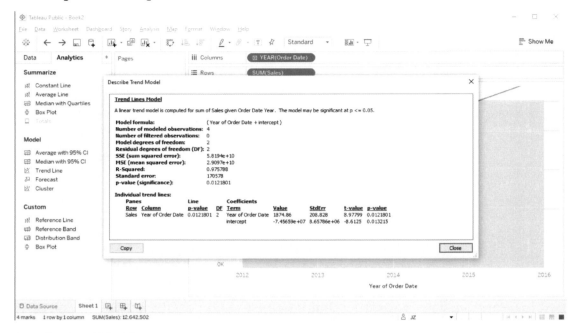

Describe Trend Model

In addition to the trend line modelling, it is possible to use Tableau analytics to forecast a 2016 sales amount. There will be a wide margin of error around the model, but it may provide additional insight for setting the 2016 goal. While it something to play with to further your understanding, it is out of scope for the exam.

As a final reference line example, below is a chart showing the average sales amount across each pane. Splitting out the data by product category, we can get a sense of which categories are driving the sales increases each year.

Pane Reference Lines

There is a lot of flexibility in using reference and trend lines in Tableau, and more information is available at the Tableau website for reference lines[21], trend lines[22], and the analytics pane[23] in general.

Create a calculated field (e.g. string, date, simple arithmetic)

When exploring data, it is common to realize an additional field may be informative in the view. Returning to the data source to retrieve or calculate this field may take more effort that in it's worth. What if the field isn't even that valuable, in the end?

Calculated fields extend the data set, without requiring you to go back to source, and they are useful to calculate ratios, segment the data, convert data types, filter results, and perform aggregations.

As an example, in our Superstore data set, we have profit and sales, but we do not have a profit ratio. We can easily create a profit ratio field using SQL-like syntax and formulas directly in Tableau.

Right-clicking on a field in the data pane brings up a drop-down menu with a sub-menu, "Create," that contains a "Calculated Field" option. Selecting "Calculated Field" pops up the calculations editor. Here you can write formulas that calculate field values, using a wide range of functions.

Calculating Profit Ratio

Inside the calculation editor, there is a small triangle on the right edge of the formula box. This is the toggle for displaying the formula list and descriptions. Clicking it expands the editor to include a help box, which displays a list of functions and their descriptions and syntax. When the screen cursor is on a function, or you start typing a function, the help box displays the formula details, including inputs and an example. If the cursor is on the field, the help box displays the field's metadata.

It is possible to create both dimensions and measures as calculated fields. For measures, it is important to mind the behavior of the fields in the worksheet. Note the AGG function around profit ratio in the row shelf.

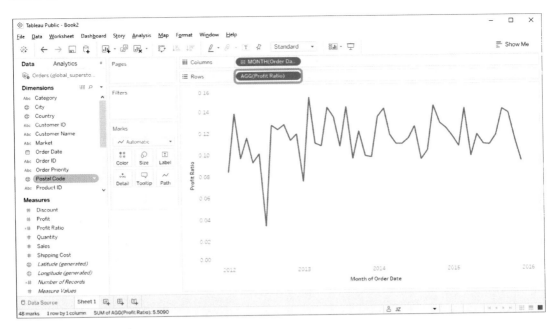

Profit Ratio by Month

The profit ratio takes the sum of profit and divides by the sum of sales. Tableau performs those calculations independently at the Viz LOD, and then divides those calculation results.

For example, if we plot profit ratio through time, using ship date, Tableau sums the profit and sales amounts for the specific period, then it divides the sum of profit by the sum of sales. Tableau indicates this nested calculation using the "AGG()" function called out above.

If we add a dimension that changes the Viz LOD, then the Profit Ratio will recalculate based on the new Viz LOD. For example, dragging category onto color, we can produce a line with the profit ratio by category.

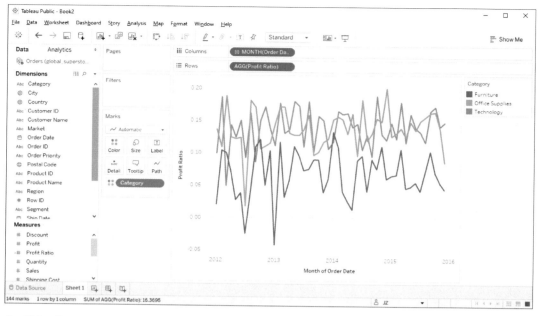

Profit by Category

Now Tableau sums the profit and sales amounts by month and category before creating the ratio. Our visual output, includes the individual profit ratio fore each category in each of the months.

Tableau also includes many logical functions, such as IF and CASE statements, that are useful when calculating dimensions to group or segment the data.

There are two very important factors to remember when working with calculations.

The first factor is performance cost. As the size of the data set increases, Tableau takes longer to generate the view, while it waits to finish running the calculations. If the calculated fields are easily pushed back to the data extraction / source, it is best do that between designing your visual and publishing it. It is especially important to move calculations to the extract process when you a calculation on an existing calculated field. Chaining together calculated fields drastically reduces Tableau's responsiveness.

The second factor is to "Please Excuse My Dear Aunt Sally!" That's a common mnemonic to help remember the PEMDAS order of operations.

1. Parenthesis

2. Exponents

3. Multiplication

4. Division

5. Addition

6. Subtraction

Tableau, like all computer calculations, follows this standard mathematical order of operations within formulas. Tableau calculates the items in parenthesis first, then the exponents, and the rest of the functions in that order. This allows for a lot of flexibility in the logic used for calculations when mastered because you can nest functions and mathematical operators in the formula.

However, this flexibility brings complexity. The more complex your calculated field becomes the more difficult it is to understand and explain, when someone else picks up your visualization or Tableau workbook.

For a deeper dive into calculations, check out the expanded information on the Tableau site[24].

Use a table calculation

Extending the calculation capability, Tableau includes functionality to produce table calculations.

Table calculations are transformations Tableau performs in the visualization. They are special calculated field types computing values within Tableau, and their scope is limited to only the measures and dimension that are present in the visualization. Table calculations exclude any data removed from the visualization by filters.

Common uses of table calculations are showing the percent of total, running totals, and rankings, and to let's look at a table of sales by category and sub-category, with totals.

Sales by Category and Sub-category

Looking at the sales table above, we can right click the Sales pill to "Add a Table Calculation."

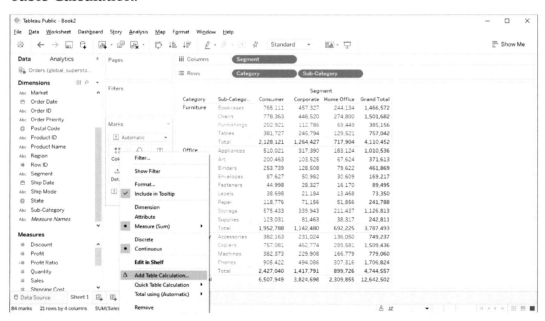

Add Table Calc

Notice below that Tableau highlights the first row of the table to indicate the calculation is by the table across. The best way to read these calculations is with ordered phrasing for the inputs:

1. For each…

2. Calculate the…

3. By the…

Table Calculation

Now, let's read the table below. (Note: First, drag the sales pill on to the table so you have the totals and the table calculation.)

For each segment Tableau calculated the percent of total by the table across the rows.

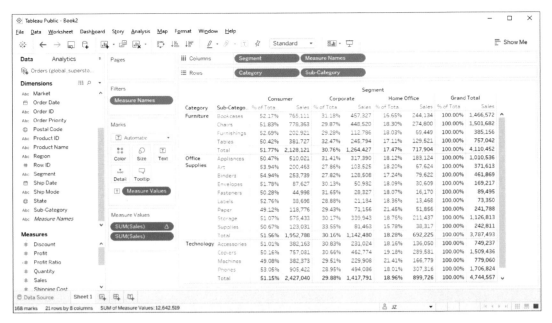

Category	Sub-Catego..	Consumer % of Tota	Sales	Corporate % of Tota	Sales	Home Office % of Tota	Sales	Grand Total % of Tota	Sales
Furniture	Bookcases	52.17%	765,111	31.18%	457,327	16.65%	244,134	100.00%	1,466,572
	Chairs	51.83%	778,363	29.87%	448,520	18.30%	274,800	100.00%	1,501,682
	Furnishings	52.69%	202,921	29.28%	112,786	18.03%	69,449	100.00%	385,156
	Tables	50.42%	381,727	32.47%	245,794	17.11%	129,521	100.00%	757,042
	Total	51.77%	2,128,121	30.76%	1,264,427	17.47%	717,904	100.00%	4,110,452
Office Supplies	Appliances	50.47%	510,021	31.41%	317,390	18.12%	183,124	100.00%	1,010,536
	Art	53.94%	200,463	27.86%	103,525	18.20%	67,624	100.00%	371,613
	Binders	54.94%	253,739	27.82%	128,508	17.24%	79,622	100.00%	461,869
	Envelopes	51.78%	87,627	30.13%	50,982	18.09%	30,609	100.00%	169,217
	Fasteners	50.28%	44,998	31.65%	28,327	18.07%	16,170	100.00%	89,495
	Labels	52.76%	38,696	28.88%	21,184	18.36%	13,468	100.00%	73,350
	Paper	49.12%	118,776	29.43%	71,156	21.45%	51,856	100.00%	241,788
	Storage	51.07%	575,433	30.17%	339,943	18.76%	211,437	100.00%	1,126,813
	Supplies	50.67%	123,031	33.55%	81,463	15.78%	38,317	100.00%	242,811
	Total	51.56%	1,952,788	30.16%	1,142,480	18.28%	692,225	100.00%	3,787,493
Technology	Accessories	51.01%	382,163	30.83%	231,024	18.16%	136,050	100.00%	749,237
	Copiers	50.16%	757,081	30.66%	462,774	19.18%	289,581	100.00%	1,509,436
	Machines	49.08%	382,373	29.51%	229,908	21.41%	166,779	100.00%	779,060
	Phones	53.05%	905,422	28.95%	494,086	18.01%	307,316	100.00%	1,706,824
	Total	51.15%	2,427,040	29.88%	1,417,791	18.96%	899,726	100.00%	4,744,557

Table Calculation with Original Value

To help understand how Tableau runs the calculation, grab a calculator, and divide the sales amount for bookcases (756,111) into the row grand total (1,466,572). Let's check your understanding with another table calculation. Below is the edit box for a different table calculation. Take a minute to read the image to your self. (For each... Compute the... By the...)

Table Calc Knowledge Check

Now that you're an expert on the table calculations, let's use then in a visual chart. Below, we have a running total table calculation. Notice that the bars are numbered to indicate the order in which the calculation runs. Try to read the chart using the phrasing from above, and then check your phrasing against the paragraph below.

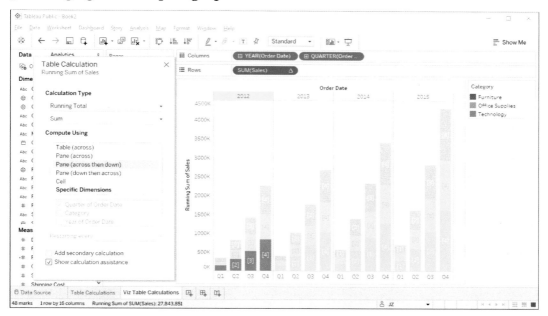

Table Calculation Chart

The table calculation in the stacked bar chart calculates a running total. Read it as: for each quarter, compute the running total by the pane across and then down. This produces a running total sales in each category by quarter of each year.

Table calculations are an excellent tool for adding layers to your visualizations. For example, placing the table calculation on the detail section of the marks card, you can display the percent of total for a value in the tool tip. This lets you highlight a categories specific portion of sales.

Table Calc on Details

Hovering over the furniture value for Q4 2012, the tool tip in the above chart tells us Furniture sales for that period were 13.064% total sales for 2012. Including table calculations in the detail, and other layers of the view, is a great way to expand the information included.

While Tableau tends to produce more graphs than tables, experimenting with tables is the best way to solidify your understanding of table calculations. Open up a data set in Tableau, and study how the visual or the table changes with each adjustment to the table calculation settings.

For more detail check out the Tableau site for an overview of table calculations[25] and for details on the different table calculation functions[26].

Level of Detail Expressions (LOD)

As we briefly covered in the overview of Tableau concepts, Tableau evaluates calculations at the Viz LOD. However, Tableau also includes the ability to calculate values at an independent level of detail. Remember that the level of detail refers to the granularity of the data presented, and Tableau sets the level of detail based on the dimension used in the view.

There are three options for calculating an independent level of detail.

- **FIXED** calculates the values based solely on dimensions in the formula. (Static)

- **INCLUDE** calculates the values based on the viz LOD, and it includes the additional dimensions specified in the formula. (Lower)

- **EXCLUDE** calculates the values based on the viz LOD; however it excludes the specified dimensions. (Higher)

Now for the syntax.

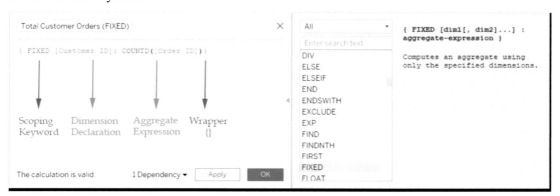

Fixed LOD Expression Syntax

The first item is the scoping keyword (FIXED, INCLUDE, and EXCLUDE). The scoping keyword determines whether the calculation has a static level of detail (FIXED), lower level of detail (INCLUDE), or higher level of detail (EXCLUDE).

In the example above, we created Total Customer Orders at a fixed LOD, using the Customer ID for the dimension declaration. Then, we specify that the Total Customer Orders should be the distinct count of Order ID. Remember that the grain of the Superstore data is a combination of Order ID and Product ID so we need to count unique orders. Otherwise, we will double count orders with multiple products on the invoice.

This fixed LOD calculation produces the total orders by Customer ID, regardless of the Viz LOD. This means if we have a filled map, for example. Total Customer Orders calculates across the entire map, ignoring the specific geography dimensions.

Furthermore, we can create a fixed level of detail with no dimension specified. Here, we have the total global orders represented as a FIXED LOD function.

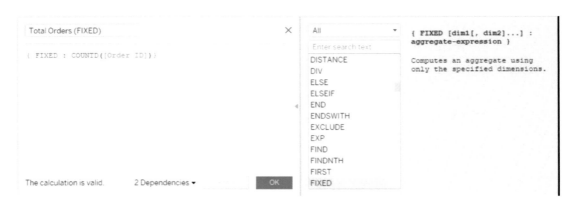

Fixed LOD Expression No Dimension Specified

It's possible to calculate the same value using a table calculation, but the table calculation will change based on filtering, whereas the FIXED LOD calculation will always show the same number irrespective of the filtering. When we bring up the map below, you will be able to see the detailed nuances between the calculations, but first, let's look at the INCLUDE scoping for the LOD calculations.

Using INCLUDE, tells Tableau to start with the viz LOD, and then use an additional dimension to perform the specified calculation.

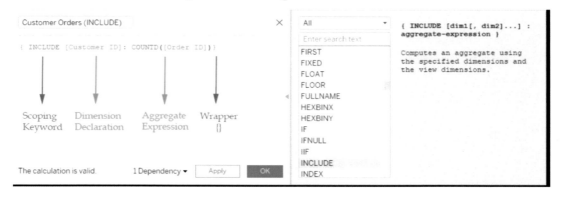

Include LOD Expression Syntax

Above, we create a metric for Customer Orders, using the INCLUDE level of detail expression. The output of this calculation will take extend the view to calculate a distinct order count at the customer level in addition to the existing viz LOD. To illustrate, let's look at a map of order volumes. The color indicates the percentage of global sales for each country, and there is additional detail when you hover the mouse cursor over a state. Follow along with the Zero to Data Viz Superstore workbook on Tableau Public[27].

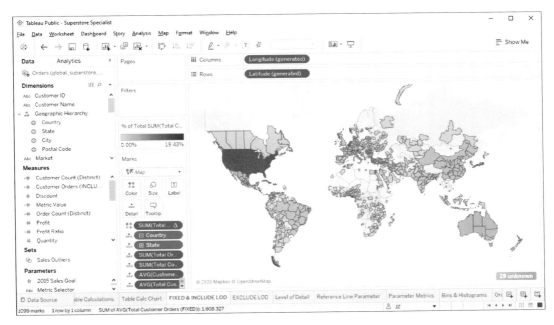

LOD Map Example

I used a fixed LOD calculation for total country orders, and then applied a table calculation so that we could see the percent of global sales for each country. Then, for illustrative purposes, I added a variety of standard expressions, FIXED LOD expressions, and INCLUDE LOD expressions. These are all used in the tool tip to walk through the calculations Tableau performs. First, you can see the total global sales and total country sales numbers using FIXED LOD expressions. The table calculation on the Total Country (Fixed) field produces the same percentage as dividing those two numbers.

Then the tool tip breaks down the customer orders using a combination of standard and INCLUDE LOD expressions. While you can often times calculate the same number using multiple standard expressions, the LOD output will be more consistent across filtering and other changes. It will also run a bit faster in many instances.

Finally, the tool tip revisits the FIXED LOD expressions to illustrate how to read the output.

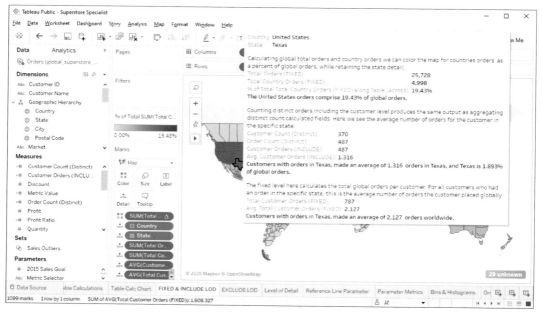

LOD Tooltip Detail

Now that we've covered the FIXED and EXCLUDE LOD expression, here is an example of common use for the EXCLUDE LOD. The first thing to consider is the syntax and how it reads for EXCLUDE vs the others. Below Tableau will calculate the sum of sales at the viz LOD excluding the sub-category dimension.

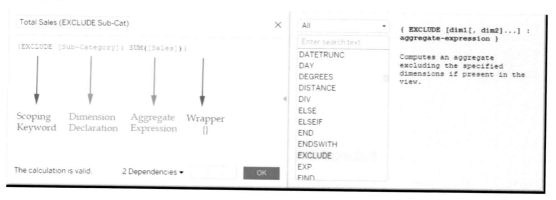

Exclude Syntax

We can plot this calculated field along with sales by sub-category to illustrate the portion of category sales accounted for by each sub-category. To start, let's create a horizontal bar chart that present the sum of sales next to the total sales LOD expression, and change the color of the sum of sales to orange.

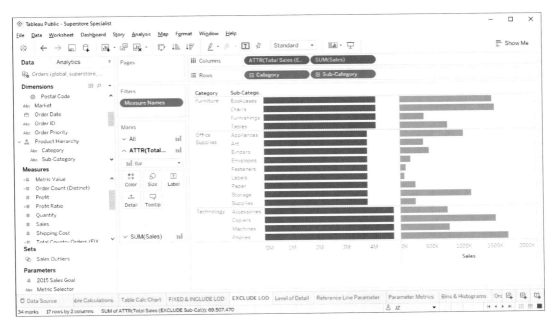

Exclude Example

Now we can see the total sales in each sub-category with the total category sales next to them. However, notice that the axis range is different so it distorts perception of the proportions. If we change this to a synchronized dual-axis chart, Tableau overlays the bars representing sub-category sales on top of the bars that exclude sub-category. This shows us total sales by category, and the proportion proportional sub-category sales. With a few additional aesthetic tweaks, we can add labels for min and max amounts for the sub-categories, as well as the total number for each category. We will cover this in more detail when we get to formatting views and workbooks, but it is useful here to illustrate the value of EXCLUDE LOD expressions. Spend a minute investigating the Label options and see how much you can logic through before reading through.

Exclude Dual Axis Overlay

Now you have a start on the level of detail expressions and their power in Tableau. This is a deeper dive than required to pass the exam, but it will help with understanding Tableau's order of operations. For the Tableau Desktop Specialist exam, you need to understand at a high level that fixed ignores the Viz LOD, INCLUDE calculates at a lower level from the Viz LOD, and EXCLUDE calculates at a higher level from the Viz LOD.

If you want to explore this topic further, here are additional resources from the Tableau website:

Tableau Help Site[28]

Tableau Whitepaper[29]

Tableau Blog[30]

Now, that we've covered the main items in the query pipeline, let's go a bit deeper on Tableau's order of operations.

The Query Pipeline

The query pipeline refers to the order Tableau processes the filters and formulas to produce visualizations. This is a similar concept to the order of operations we discussed regarding calculated fields, Tableau processes the data in a mostly linear order, but there are some components that run simultaneously.

When Tableau renders a view, it runs queries to fetch the data for the metrics in the view, and it runs the queries in the sequential order depicted below. The blue boxes are the primary processes, and the orange are the processes that sit in between them.

Tableau's Order of Operations

Much like the order of operations in the calculated fields section, understanding Tableau's query pipeline allows for a lot of awesome customization. The order of operations is also a common cause when the view output doesn't match the intended design. Also, understanding this order of operations provides more flexibility with the Tableau views.

For example, if you add a filter for top N and a specific geography, Tableau applies them simultaneously. To work this out, let's return to our example from the section on how to add a context filter in "Organize Data and Apply Filters."

The Texas state sales manager wants to monitor our biggest customers in her area to learn why they buy more. Let's add the context filter we used for Texas, the top N customer filter, and create a bar chart this time.

Top 10 Texas Customers by Sales

Now, let's extend this chart to include some more details. Add a dual axis measure for total sales as a percent of total, and then we can add a total sales LOD expression excluding customer name to the detail. With these, the viewer can see the numerator and denominator of the table calculation. Next, we will add two reference lines. One for average sales of the top 10 customers in Texas, and another for the median sales. Finally, let's color the chart using customer segment.

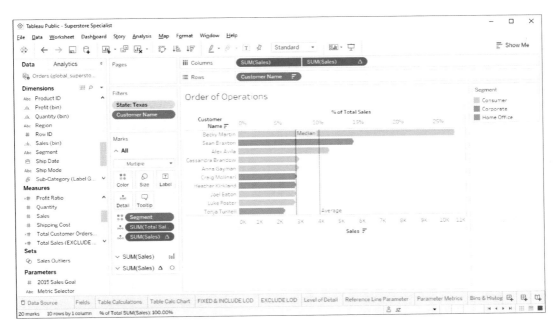

Top 10 Texas Customer Sales

Before we cover the order of operations for this chart, notice that it highlights some interesting facts for the Texas sales manager to consider.

The consumer segment makes up the majority of our top 10. Logically, one might expect business to spend more on office supplies than consumers. Also of note is the fact that the majority of the top 10 sit right around the median sales value for the group. This is a good chart to inform where the sales manager may want to investigate how to move those customers up to the average for the group, or perhaps how to convert customers outside of the top 10 to look more like this group.

Now, take a minute to review the chart, and try to assess the order tableau processed the data. Then compare your assessment to the labelled view below.

Order of Operations - Top 10 Texas Customers

Understanding the order of operations is one of the skills that separates analysts and the quality of the dashboards. Exploiting the query pipeline can improve performance, the ability to layer multiple levels of information, and consequently, the usefulness of the visualizations you create.

For additional detail and examples, check out the Tableau website[31] and the user community forums[32].

Add a parameter

Parameters are placeholders for values. Inputting or selecting a parameter value allows Tableau to use that value in reference lines, filters, and calculations. Parameters are a concept used widely in programming and modelling.

In software programming, parameters are often passed to functions to set the scope or behavior. For example, a function that represents the turning of a car, might take a direction parameter that takes the values "left" or "right."

In Tableau, parameters make workbooks more interactive and dynamic. Users can set parameter values with text input, or list selection, and the workbook responds to those values. Parameters are a great way to reuse the space on a dashboard or visualization because they have the ability to make most aspects of the view dynamic and responsive to user input. Tableau parameters are useful for setting reference values, driving calculations, filtering, and more.

Creating a parameter is similar to creating a calculated field, and then the parameter control functions much like the filter control. Once a parameter value is set, it can be used in text fields, calculations, reference lines, filters, and elsewhere throughout the view.

Reference Line Parameter

For example, if management wants to track running total of sales against a 3 scenario-based targets, high growth, moderate growth, and low growth. We can create a bar chart with the running total of sales for 2015, and then add a parameter to set a reference line based on the selected scenario.

Create Parameter

Here are the four steps to create the 2015 Sales Goals parameter:

1. Click the drop-down menu (circled) in the data pane and select "Create Parameter."

2. Tableau pops up the dialogue box, where we set the values for the parameter.

3. The parameter should be a float, and change the allowable values to a list. (The create parameter box will expands for list entry, as pictured below.)

4. Add the three items to the list, and the final create parameter box should match the following picture.

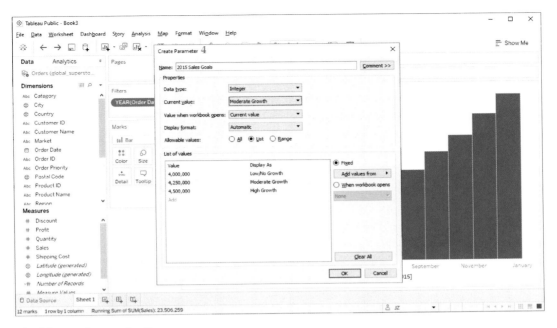

Final Create Parameter Box

After clicking "OK," the parameter shows up in a new section of the data pane. Right-click the parameter, and select "Show Parameter Control" to add it to the view. The parameter control appears on the right side of the visualization, where the filter controls display. You can drag both the filter and parameter controls to other locations in the worksheet view, if for example, you prefer them nearer to the marks card.

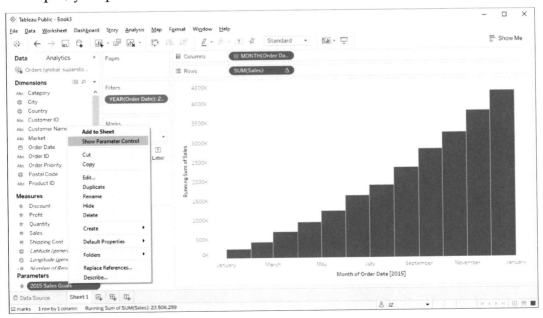

Show Parameter Control

At this point, the parameter control does not affect the view. We need to add a reference line, with its value set to the parameter value. Then the parameter control will move the reference line in the view. Drag the reference line into the view from the analytics pane, and set drop it on the SUM(Sales) across the table. This will pop up the edit reference line box pictured below, where you select the parameter, instead of the default SUM(Sales) value. I also recommend setting the label option to value.

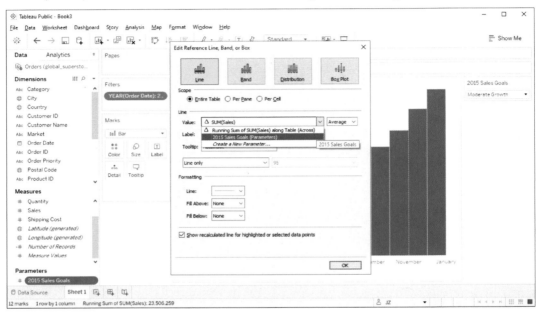

Edit Reference Line to Use Parameter

After you click "OK," the parameter control will move the reference line on the graph. Pictured below is the final visual.

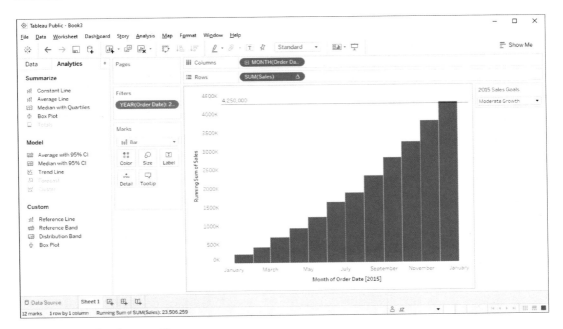

Paremeterized Reference Line

In addition to adjusting reference lines we can use parameters as inputs for calculations.

Parameters in Calculations

Two common calculations based on parameters values are scenario analysis and dynamic metric selection. Remember, during the combined axis charts, we discussed a reduction in shipping costs having a direct impact on profit. Using a parameter, we can allow the viewers to explore scenarios based on an estimated reduction in shipping costs.

Create a parameter called "Est. Shipping Savings (%)," and set to an integer starting at 0, ending at 20, and with a step size of 1.

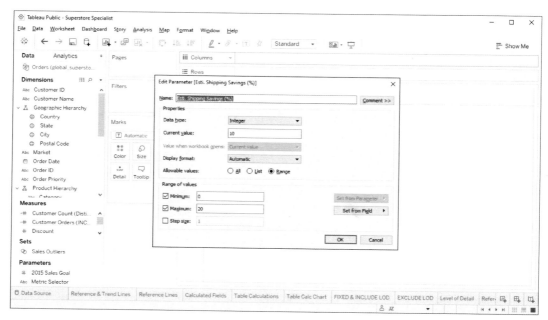

Est. Shipping Savings (%) Parameter

Now, create a calculated field called "Ship Cost" that equals the actual shipping costs reduced by the percentage specified in the parameter selection.

Calculated Ship Cost Using Parameter

The final calculation is the adjusted profit. Starting with the profit value add in the dollar reduction in shipping costs based on the estimated savings.

Adjusted Profit Using the Parameter

The final step is to show the parameter control and create the combined area graph from the basic charts section. However, instead of using the actual profit and shipping cost, use the adjusted profit and ship costs. Now, the area graph adjusts based on the savings estimate input int the parameter.

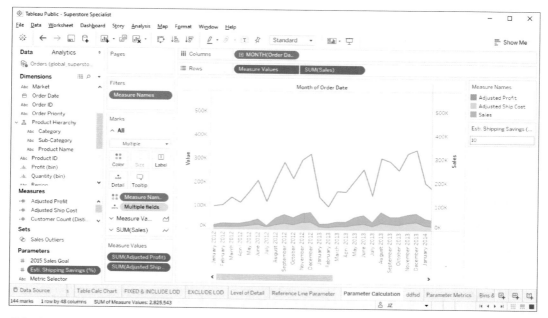

Shipping Cost Scenarios Using Parameter

Another way to use parameter values in calculations is to create "If statement' calculations that return metric values based on a parameter selection. Creating a new parameter named metric selector, we can list out metrics, and then the viewer controls which metrics the visual displays. This is an efficient use of space. Rather than having to reload a new page or click to a different section, the viewer, selects a parameter value, and their current view displays new information.

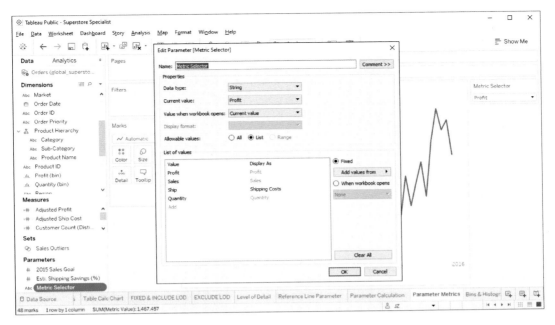

Create Metric Select

Next, create a calculated field, "Metric Value," and write an "IF statement" that returns the measure value that corresponds to the parameter selection.

Create Metric Value

Now we have a measure that we can add to the rows or columns shelf, and the measure used changes based on the selection in the metric selector. First add Ship Date to the columns shelf, then add Metric Value to the rows shelf, and finally right-click the Metric Selector parameter to select "Show Parameter Control." Next, we will right click the y-axis (vertical), and delete the axis title text.

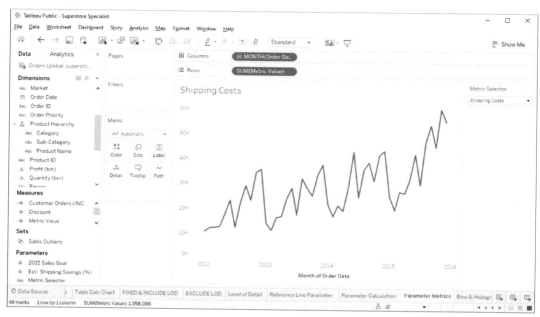

Metric Selection Parameter Visual

Notice that the worksheet title matches the Metric Selector. As mentioned above, parameter values can be used in text values.

1. Right click the worksheet title

2. Select "Edit Title"

3. Delete ""

4. Click the "Insert" drop-down

5. Select <Parameters.Metric Selector> and click OK.

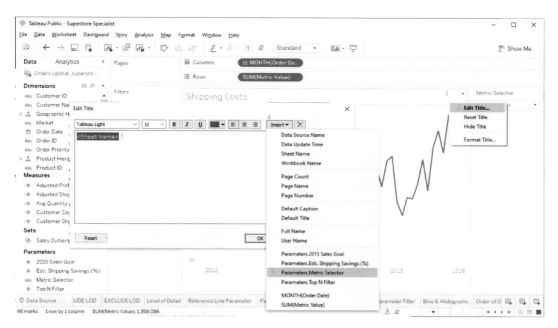

Edit Sheet Title

Filtering with a Parameter

As a final example, we can use a parameter value when filtering. Here we will use s parameter to filter on a single data source, but parameters are also useful for filtering across multiple datasources without the need to link them together with a blend or a join.

We will start with a crosstab that includes the customer sales by category, using the market and order date as context filters.

Once you have the crosstab, create a parameter input that takes an integer to use as N in a top N filter.

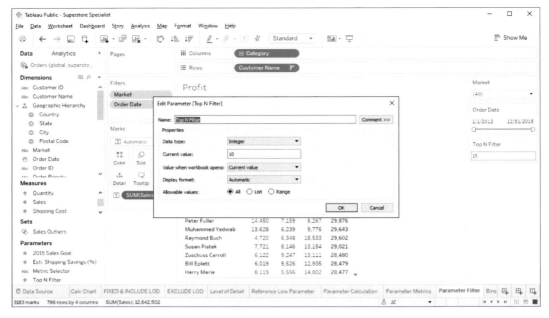

Create Top N Parameter

Next, add Customer name to the filter card, and go to the top N settings. Here, you can select the parameter value instead of the numeric default under "By field." Then, click OK.

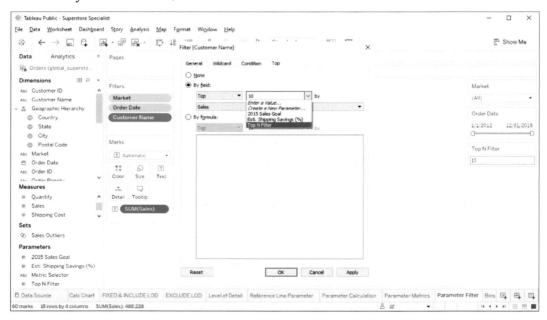

Add Customer Name Filter

The final crosstab updates based on the context filter values, and then displays the relevant top N customers by sales. The viewer can select the number of customers they wish to see, and with no extra work from the visualization analyst.

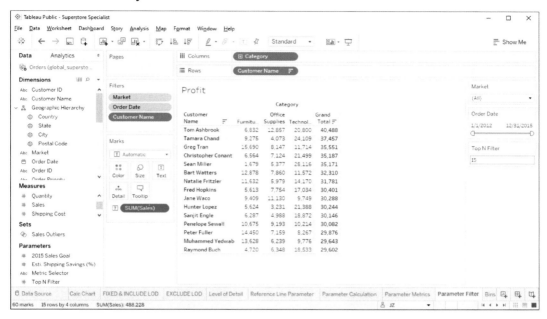

Filtering with Parameter Value

As you can see, parameters are extremely versatile, and they add a lot of value, with respect to making visuals more dynamic and interactive. Parameters will likely show up on the exam as theoretical questions, and they are an essential skill for creating dynamic, interactive dashboards.

Using the metric selector example above, create a vertical bar chart that uses the category and segment dimensions to segment the different metrics. We will use this metric breakdown later when we create a dashboard.

Use bins and histograms

Creating bins is a technique for converting continuous measures into discrete dimensions. Think of the age ranges commonly used on surveys (<20, 20-29, 30-39, 40-49, 50-59, 60+). Rather than specify the persons exact age, the ages are binned into relevant ranges, and the ranges might vary based on the survey. The selection of the start and end age for each bin is critical to the interpretation of the data, and we will talk more about setting this bin size shortly.

In Tableau, generating histograms is the most a common use of binned variables. More broadly, analysts use data binning to deal with outliers, missing data values, minor data errors, or to simplify the data set for summarization and reporting.

Bins come with a distortion risk because they can easily misrepresent behaviors and segmentation, if improperly constructed. Creating bins requires special attention because as you will see it can radically impact the interpretation of data.

Normal Distribution Overview

To add context, let's start with a histogram of the normal curve, often mentioned as the bell curve because of its shape.

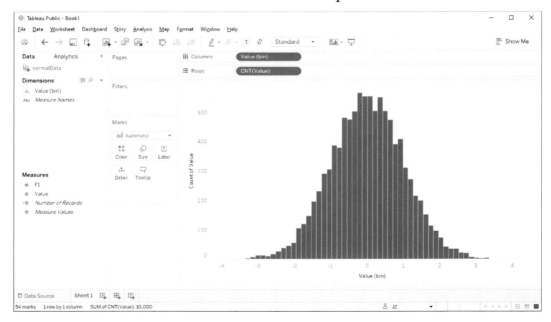

Normal Distribution Histogram

The above histogram is a randomly generated set of numbers with a mean of 0 and a standard deviation of 1. In statistics, the name for this specific curve is the normal distribution. Histograms illustrate the distribution of data, which refers to where the values fall with respect to the mean (average) value. Notice the average value of 0 is the center of the graph.

The normal distribution follows a set of statistical rules with respect to probability, and this conformity enables us make assumptions about patterns and behavior. If you look at the graph above, you can see that the majority of the observations fall around the average value of 0. Based on proven statistical formulas, we know that 95% of the observations fall within 2 standard deviations of the mean for a normal curve.

Standard deviation measures the distance of each observation from the mean, and these differences in aggregate indicate the width of histogram. A higher standard deviation indicates the values are spread out over a wider range, which produces a wider histogram.

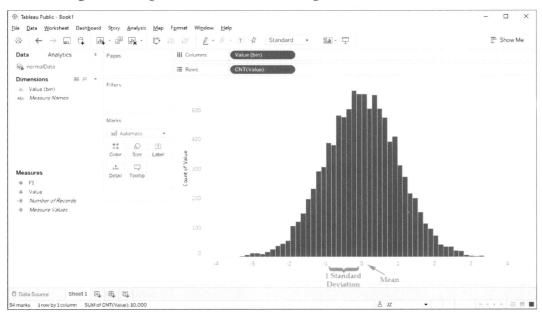

Mean & Std. Deviation

In the normal distribution above, the mean is 0 and the standard deviation is 1. This means that on average the observations are +/- 1 from 0. To be more specific, 68% of the observations fall within 1 standard deviation, 95% within 2 standard deviations of the mean (1.95996 if you want to be more exact), and 99.7% observations within 3 standard deviations.

Using the standard deviation we can now create a confidence interval 95% is the confidence interval. Referring back to our histogram, you can see that most of the observations fall between -2 and 2. Based on the normally distributed data, we are 95% confident the next data point generated in this data set will fall in that range. This is one of many statistical inferences made possible from analysis of normally distributed data.

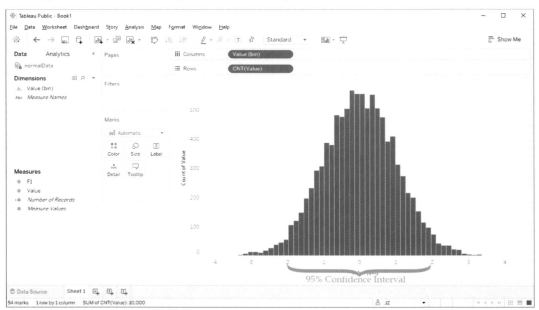

95% Confidence Interval

Working with real world data, histograms are used to compare the distribution of a data set to the shape of the normal distribution. The more closely a distribution matches the normal distribution, the more likely the data behaves in accordance with the properties of a normal distribution. This is very useful for making predictions.

Statistical analysis relies heavily on assumptions about the data. Given the characteristics of a data set, there are different assumptions and techniques that apply. A histogram is such a powerful tool because it allows an viewer to assess the distribution of a data set in a quick glance. For a team building, or monitoring, a predictive model, the histogram is an essential visual.

Creating a Histogram

Grab the normal data from the companion site, and we will create a histogram for the normal distribution, before exploring the global superstore data.

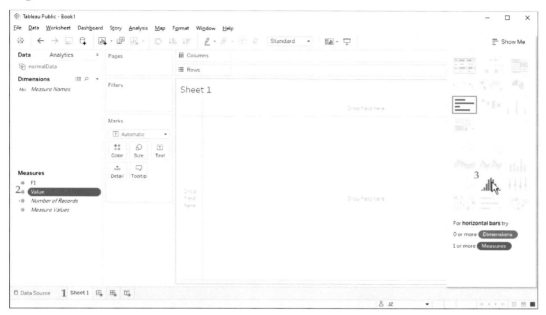

Show Me - Histogram

1. Open the normal data in Tableau, and go to Sheet 1.
2. Select the "Value" field in the measures section of the data pane.
3. Open the "Show Me" menu, and click the histogram icon.
4. Tableau generates the histogram for the normal distribution.

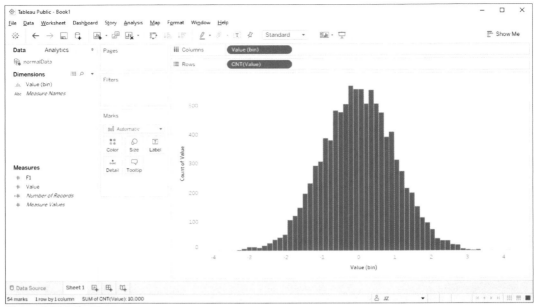

Normal Distribution

Notice that this creates a field in the dimensions section of the data pane, Value (bin), and that it is a green pill, which indicates a continuous variable. We can manually create the histogram by placing a continuous binned variable on the columns shelf and the count of observations on the rows shelf.

Create & Edit Bins

If we right click this new binned dimension, and select edit. The "Edit Bins" dialogue box displays the current bin size, and it has 4 additional data points, Min, Max, Diff, and CntD.

By default, Tableau uses a field's min, max, distinct number of records, and the difference between the min and max to estimate the bin size, or bin width. Tableau uses a formula to calculate the number of bins and then divides the difference by that number. The "Edit Bins" dialogue box includes all 4 of those values at the bottom for reference.

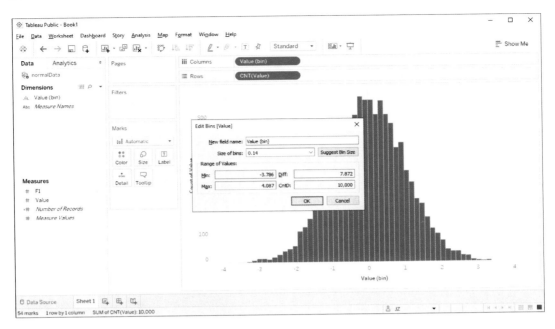

Edit Bin

The bin size is critical because it hides information if the bins are set incorrectly. Using random normal data, change the bin size to 0.20 from the Tableau default of 0.14, and the graph changes. The vertical axis increases to 800, and instead of 54 bins, there are now only 38 bins.

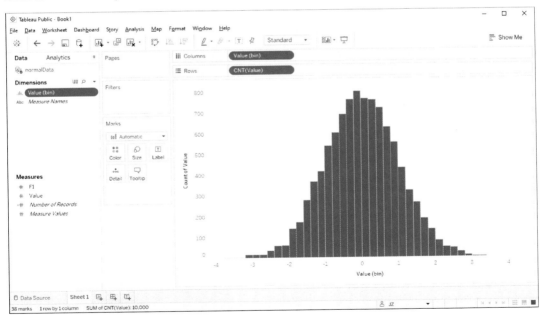

Adjusted Bin Size

In order to demonstrate just how much this can impact the histogram, let's set the bin size to 1.00. Now, we have a completely different graph, with only 9 bins. With a normal distribution, we can distinguish a boxier bell shape, but there is likely hidden information in the wider bins.

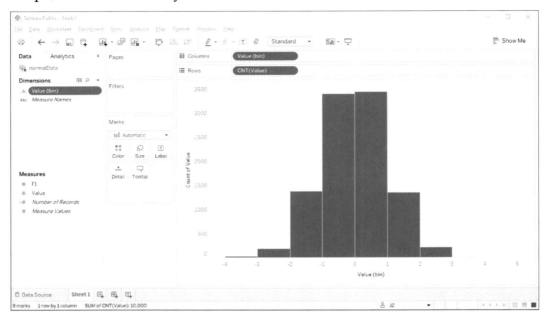

Distorted Histogram

As you can see setting the bins impacts the interpretation of the data. While this example used the default bin created by Tableau, we can also create our own bins. Simply right click any continuous, numeric field, and select the "Bins" option under "Create" in the drop-down menu. Tableau will open the "Edit Bins" dialogue box, with the suggested bin size populated. Feel free to play around with the bin sizes. You can always click the "Suggest Bin Size" button reset the bin sizing to the default.

Global Superstore Example

Returning to the superstore data set let's look at a histogram for quantity ordered. Use the "Show Me" menu to create a histogram for quantity.

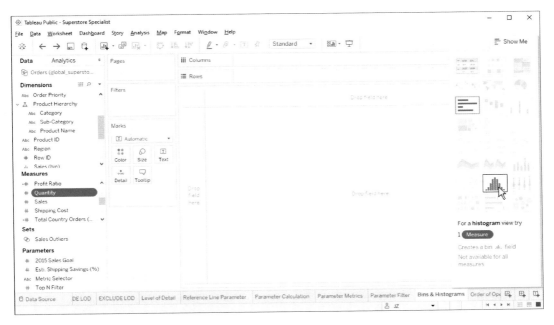

Create Quantity Histogram

Tableau produces the default histogram, which illustrates a positively skewed distribution. The skewness refers to the size of the tails. Here, the tail extends to the right side of the histogram. This makes sense because quantity is always going to be positive because orders require a positive quantity. The positive skew tells us the data is NOT normally distributed.

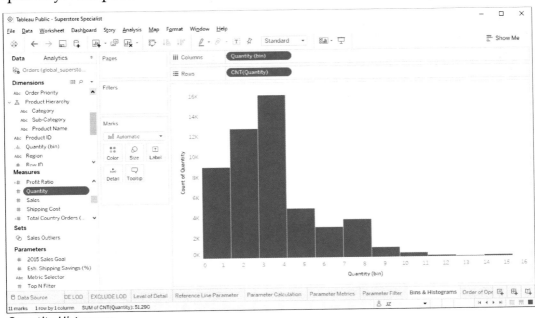

Quantity Histogram

Further examining the histogram of quantity ordered, we see that the quantity tends to be 1-3 for most product orders. Also, notice that the tail is very thin at quantities greater than 10. In a wider distribution we might adjust the bins, but since the max quantity fits, we will leave it be.

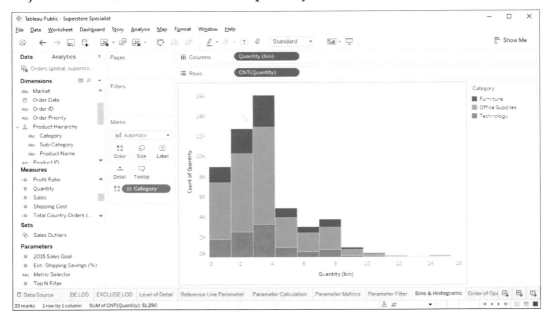

Color & Default Bin Size

Beyond adjust the bin size, it is possible to added color and other layers to the histogram to provide further detail. Coloring the bars by Category, we see that most of the high quantity items are office supplies. This seems logical, given the office supplies are less reusable than furniture.

What else do you notice about this chart? Are there any other dimensions you're curious about? Is the default bin size of 1.39 the most useful? Before we move on to "Sharing Insights," let's look at a bin size of 1. Given the smaller range of quantities ordered, this view is easier to interpret because the bins align more consistently to actual order quantities. The defaults in Tableau are quick and helpful, but it is always a good idea to take a few minutes to explore other options.

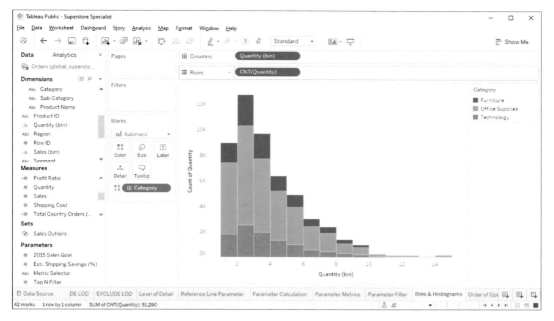

Quantity Bin Size = 1

Now you have the tools and knowledge to explore and analyze data with Tableau, it is time to learn how to the share the insights you discover.

Sharing Insights

Learning outcome

A good story needs to be told, and while Tableau is an excellent tool for analyzing data, sharing insights is how you drive outcomes. Sharing insights provides confirmation that the outcomes from business decisions are positive, and where we can focus to continue improving. This final section covers the mechanics and a little design theory so you can tell the data's story in an impactful way. formatting, dashboards, stories, interactive elements, and extending your visualization beyond Tableau.

By the end of this section you will understand:

- how to format your visualization
    - color, bolding, fonts, shapes, and marks
- how to create and modify a dashboard
    - interactive and explanatory elements
    - construct actions when users interact with the dashboard
    - create a mobile layout from your dashboard
    - create story using dashboards and visuals
- how to share your work as an image file

Format view for presentation

In a professional context, the deadlines and work volume often mean formatting and presentation receive the least attention. However, the formatting is critical for leading the viewer through the data's story in an unbiased way. The use of colors and sizing can easily misrepresent information. By default Tableau handles much of this, but working in a company's unique branding and design aesthetic can be worth a little extra effort. With Tableau, you have the ability to customize almost everything, by simply right-clicking the object and selecting "Format," but best practice is a top-down approach. Setting the formatting in the following order cascades the settings through the workbook, reducing the number of formatting options you must specify.

1. Set the workbook formatting

2. Adjust the worksheet options

3. Work through the tooltips and titles.

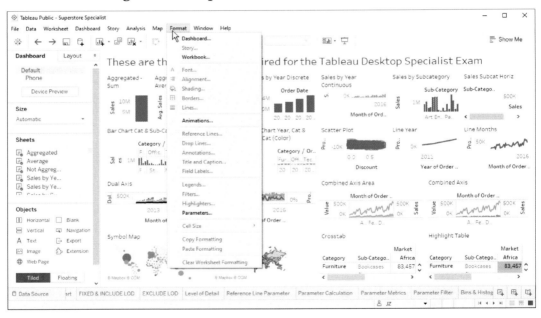

Accessing the format menu

While format options are available by right-clicking most Tableau objects, the format menu is the starting place for our top-down approach. The drop-down menu contains different options, depending on your location in the workbook, and the object selection within the view. This menu also contains one of the differences between Tableau Public and the full desktop version. The full version contains a workbook theme option, and allows you to specify a theme that corresponds to earlier versions of Tableau. I recommend leaving it set to default, unless you work in an organization with a large number of legacy Tableau workbooks.

Selecting workbook from the format menu, produces a formatting pane in the side-bar. The settings available in the formatting pane will vary based on the selected object for formatting (i.e. workbook, worksheet, story, legend, etc.).

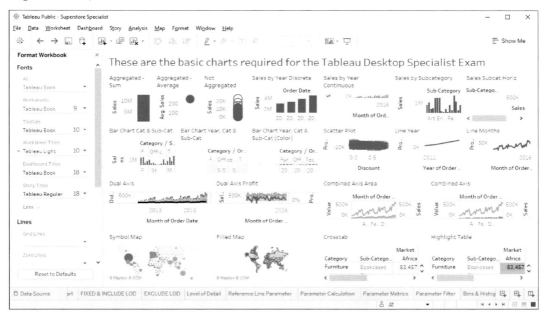

Format Pane

Adjustments made in the Format Workbook pane cascade through all the sheets, dashboards and stories. Useful settings to consider here are grid lines, fonts (size, type, and color), and line (size, shape, and color).

When adjusting fonts, colors, shapes and sizes there are a few things to consider. * Where will viewer see the visuals? On the web, in the Tableau application, or as an exported image? * What size will the view be? * What device will the viewer use?

Optimal font and color selection changes depending on the output, the story, and the context. Make sure to think about how your formatting leads the viewer through the visualization. This is your opportunity to ensure the message comes through clearly. An important metric to keep in mind is the data-ink ratio. This concept comes from one of the original experts in data visualization, Edward Tufte in his 1983 book, "The Visual Display of Quantitative Information."

Imagine the view is printed on paper, and then consider whether the ink on the page is conveying information. A data-ink ratio of 100% means every piece of ink conveys information. Any markings that are not conveying information are superfluous and distracting. Taking this to the screen the only reason a pixel should be there is because it conveys information. Grid lines, borders, and other non-data markings should be used sparingly.

Continuing to drill down from the workbook level we will look at formatting options for various elements of a dashboard, worksheet, and story. At a high level, there are options for the canvas, controls, legends and marks. Selecting a worksheet in the dashboard, and clicking the format menu, brings up a new set of options.

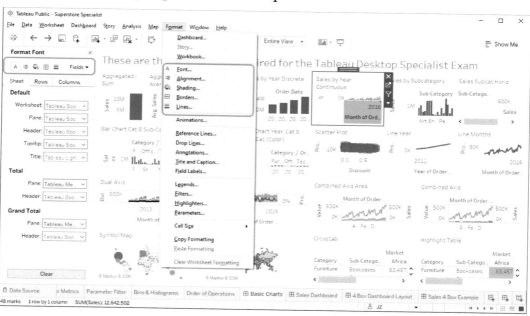

Worksheet Format Options

When formatting a worksheet, there are options present for the different elements of the chart, and the icons next to each one are present in both the drop-down menu and the format pane. Once the format pane is visible, clicking the different buttons will change the pane so you can edit those settings. The options are:

- Font which changes the type face for the elements of the worksheet specified in the format pane

- Alignment changes the text horizontal and vertical alignment and direction, as well as the text-wrapping

- Shading changes the background fill for the different columns, rows, and panes within the worksheet

- Borders is where you adjust color and size of the border between columns, rows, and panes

- Lines is where you adjust the various lines in the view, grid lines, reference lines, trend lines, axis, and so on

- Fields is a drop-down that takes you to the field-specific formatting based on the field's location in the view

Use color

Most of the above format options will have the ability to adjust the color, and Tableau is quite flexible in this regard. With this flexibility comes great responsibility. Misuse of color can be distracting at best, and the wrong colors easily mislead the viewer. For example, red tends to indicate a negative context compared to the positive context implied by green. Additionally, overuse of color or placing certain colors next to each other will produce distracting visuals that dilute the information and story.

Color from the Format Pane

Within the format pane, clicking most format options brings up a color palette for the selected item. The color menu is consistent across most objects, but there is a special color menu in the marks card to set colors based on field values. For now, let's look at the color options for fonts, lines, and other aesthetic components of the visualization.

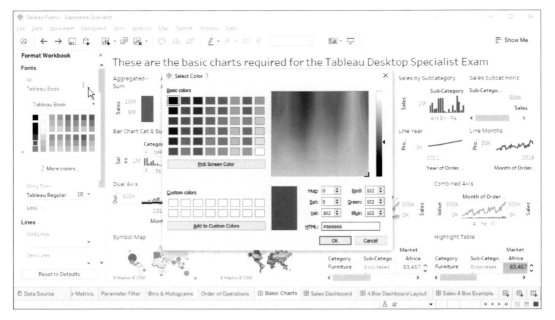

Font Color

Above, is the expanded color menu for setting the font color of all fonts in the workbook.

1.   Click the dropdown next to the Tableau Book

2.   Select one of the displayed colors, or click "More Colors"

3.   Use the "Select Color" menu to specify any desired color.

   •   The "Pick Screen Color" button grabs any color on the screen when you hover the mouse cursor over any object within Tableau or another visible application.

Color Formatting for Marks

Changing the colors for the visualization's marks is probably the most common use of Tableau's color options. When there are not too many members in a dimension, it may be useful to use a specific color for each of the dimensions. Below is the chart with annual sales targets, and you can see that the segment dimension being dragged to the colors tile in the marks card.

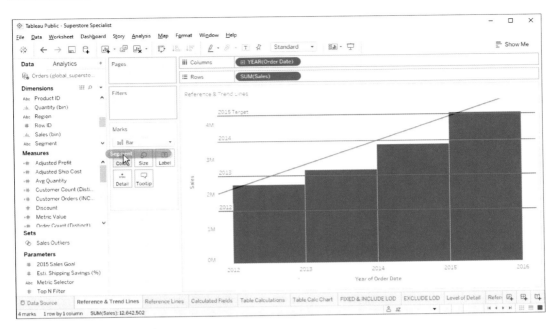

Color Marks with Dimension

This will use Tableau's default color scheme to produce a stacked bar chart with a color for each segment, consumer, corporate, and home office. While this is useful, the blue, orange and red were also the colors for category in many of the charts we created.

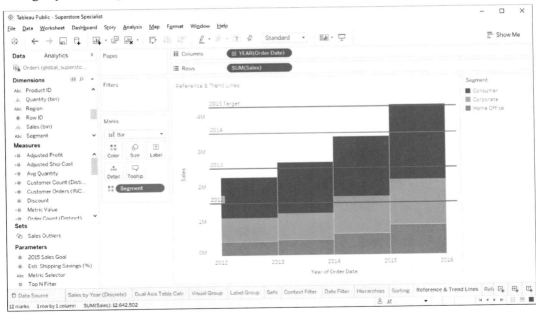

Colored Marks with Dimension

To avoid confusion, we can change the colors assigned to each member of the dimension. This will let us keep consistency throughout the workbooks and dashboards so the viewer knows that the dark blue indicates furniture, light blue is office supplies, and red is technology. Let's change the colors here for the segment values.

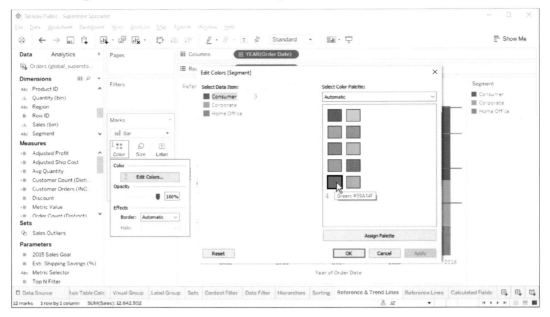

Marks Color Palette

1. Click the color tile on the marks card.

2. Click edit edit colors.

3. Click the dimension value.

4. Click the color you want to assign.

Repeat those steps for each dimension member, and click apply if you want to preview it. If you are happy with the assigned colors, click "OK" to exit the color menu.

Alternatively, you can set the default color properties for a dimension using the drop-down menu that appears when right-clicking in the data pane. Setting the colors through the default properties ensures the dimension values display using the same color throughout the workbook.

When setting mark colors in the worksheet, or with default properties, Tableau includes a large selection of color palettes. Click the drop-down menu for "Select Color Palette," and choose from the loaded palettes. Once you select a new palette, the assign palette button to map colors to the dimension members by default, or you can assign them manually, by following the steps above.

Use a color palette

You can create your own color palettes, by editing the "Preferences.tps" file. Table creates this file during installation, and puts it in the "My Tableau Repository" folder on Windows. It is a nice touch to leverage a company's brand colors in the data visualizations. This requires a small bit of xml coding, but you can get by with tweaking one of the many custom palettes shared online. You can also set custom color ranges using the preferences file.

Tableau uses color ranges to color marks based on continuous values, whereas the palettes above apply to discrete values.

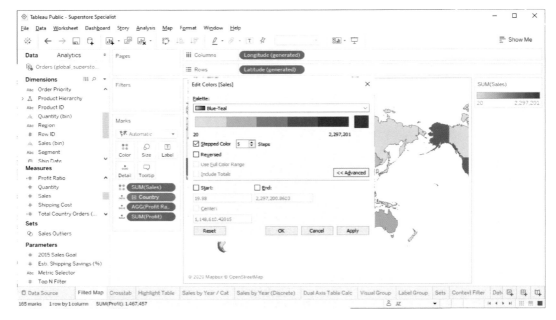

Color range for continuous values

Let's return tot he chloropleth map example from the previous section. Dragging the sales measure onto the color tile filled in the map with a range of blue color. Clicking the color tile, and selecting "Edit Colors' you can modify the presentation of the color range. Notice the color range in the edit menu compared to the map legend. Checking the"Stepped Color" box creates a discrete number of colors from the range. You can also reverse the order, and set custom values for the start, end, and center of the range. This is helpful when you have a wide range of values with a long tail on either side.

Finally, Tableau can set different colors for specific analytics elements, such as reference and trend lines.

Format from tooltip

The worksheet formatting includes reference and trend line options, but those worksheet settings apply to the color of all lines added to the worksheet. Tableau has additional capability to set the color of individual analytics marks. As always, you can right-click and select "Format" from the dropdown menu. However, you can also select the analytics object in the view, and its tooltip will include a format button that brings up the formatting pane.

In the above example, I set the reference lines to green for the years where the target was met, and red for the year the company missed the sales target.

A final note on color

Readability is the most important metric. Adding too much color can distract from the message, and adding certain color combinations may confuse interpretation.

Be conscious of preconceptions associated with color, and the sensitivity. When reporting illness for example, think of how you would feel to be labeled red on a graph because you were unwell, and if it's death black is a bit more respectful (in the western world anyway.) The cultural and other impacts of color play a big part in the ease with which viewers can read your information.

Beyond the selection of color itself, opacity is another great feature to consider. When a plot is particularly dense, reducing the opacity provides an indicator for density because it makes the marks more transparent. The areas with a dense collection of plots will show up darker.

Tableau can use any available colors that a computer can produce, and as I mentioned earlier, there is capability to edit the preferences file to create custom color palettes[33].

Use bolding and selecting fonts

Bolding is a way to provide emphasis on text, and it refers to the weight of the lettering. A bold font is thicker, and stands out from the rest of the text.

Some text elements in Tableau, like titles, have their own text editing boxes, and others rely on the format pane. In addition to color, the format pane contains options for font selection and styling. You can set the size, color, alignment, and style. Returning to the format pane, you can adjust the font settings for the workbook elements. Here we will edit the field labels on the reference and trend lines chart.

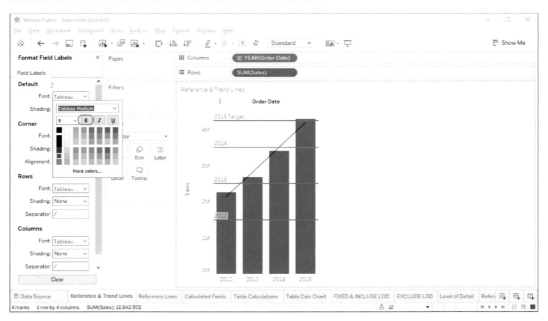

Bold from the format pane

1. Right click the field label in the viz, and select format.

2. Click the font drop down, and click the circles bold icon.

Clicking the "B" button applies bold formatting to the field label. Note that not all fonts have a bold option. Typically, fonts with a style word in their name have little no visible style change. For example, Tableau Light does not change radically with bolding, and Tableau Bold is already bold. Wherever, there is an option to set the font style (Bold, Italics, Underline), there is typically a drop-down list to select a font, and you can see the list of fonts with styles in their names there.

Additionally, the font selector and bold button show up in the edit box for tool tips, labels and other text elements. Anywhere there is text, there is an option to bold the text.

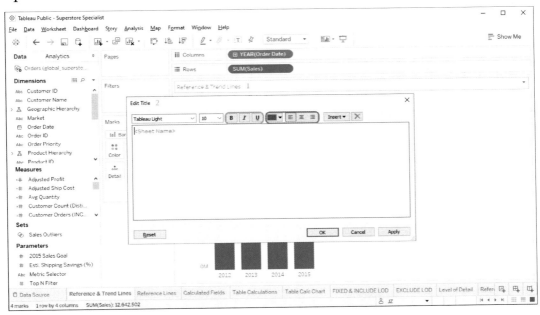

Edit Box Bold

1. Right click the text object, in this case title, and select "Edit Title."

2. The Edit Title box pops up, and there are a variety of font settings, along with space to create custom text.

   - Clicking the buttons circled in orange applies bolding, italics, and underlining

   - Clicking the options in blue adjusts color and alignment

Use shapes

Shapes are a versatile formatting and design tool in Tableau. Shapes serve as an aesthetic layer to include more information in a chart, and they can also be powerful design element. For example, I've seen Olympic graphs that use the logos from each of the Olympics as marks on a timeline, and infographics that use bar charts to fill various icons. These custom shapes are out of scope for the Tableau desktop exam, but we can still leverage the built-in shapes to customize our charts.

For example, shapes on a scatter plot are a great way to add another dimension. Returning to our scatter plot from the basic charts section, we can use shapes and color to display the product category and segment. To start bring up the profit vs. discount scatterplot, drag the category dimension onto color, and set the opacity to 50%. Now, let's investigate our shape options.

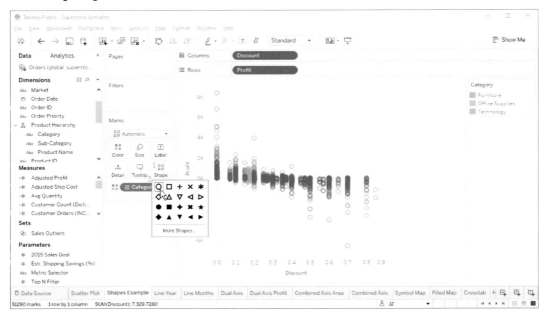

Changing Shapes

1. Click the shapes tile in the marks card

2. Click the circle outline to assign that shape to the marks in the scatterplot

    • Clicking "More Shapes" will bring up an "Edit Shape" box, similar to the "Edit Color" box

With the color set to be fairly transparent, the open circles give us an indication of the density. Cluster of circles appear as a darker color because the marks overlap. Additionally, we can use shapes in conjunction with a dimension to display different segments of the data. Let's use the segment dimension to illustrate this, by dragging the field onto the shapes tile in the mark card.

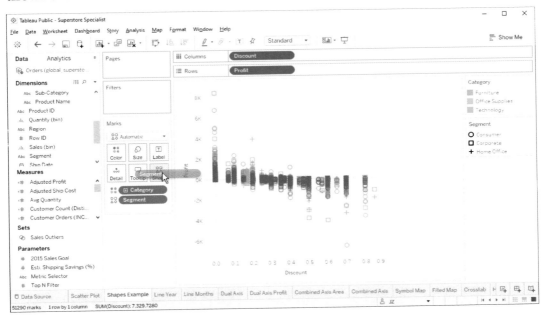

Shapes Dimension

Now the shape and color combination tells the viewer instantly which segment and category combination the mark represents. With a dimension assigned to shapes, clicking the shapes tile, bring s up the "Edit Shapes" box. Here you can specify which shape applies to each dimension member.

Edit Shapes

Furthermore, clicking the "Select Shape Palette" drop-down list shows the different options for shapes, beyond the default shapes in the above image.

While it is beyond the scope of the Tableau Desktop Specialist exam, it is possible to create custom shape palettes using image files saved to your local computer.

1. Create a new sub-folder in the "My Tableau Repository" directory on your computer.

2. Save the image files that you want to use as shapes in the newly created folder.

3. Next time you start Tableau, the palette should appear in the shapes palette selector labeled with the folder name.

Now that our scatter plot has the color and mark shape set, let's add another layer and learn about mark size.

Change size of marks

In addition to color and shape, we can set the size of the marks. The first marks adjustment is simply making the existing marks larger or smaller using the size slider.

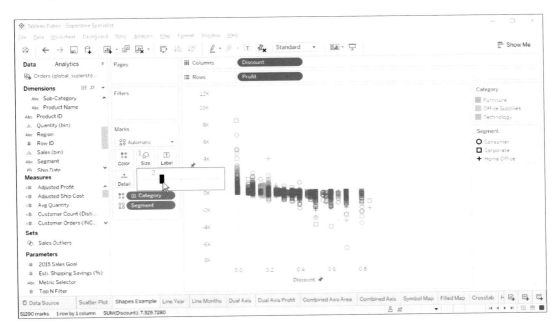

Size Slider

1.   First click the size tile on the marks card.

2.   Drag the slider left to decrease size and to the right to increase size

This adjustment increases and decreases the size of all marks the same amount. However, Tableau can also set the mark size based on a field value. There are subtle differences depending on whether the field used is discrete or continuous. Similar to color, the legend for an continuous values indicates ranges that apply to different sizes, and the discrete values have a one to one size mapping. Simply drag the field onto the size tile as pictured below.

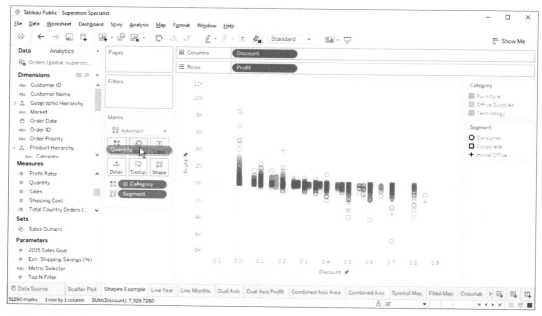

Sizing with values

Dragging the quantity field to the size tile, Tableau uses quantity to scale the size of the visualizations marks, and the view illustrates the segment, category, or quantity for each mark. If we wish to adjust the sizing. We click the size legend, drop-down, and use the "Edit Sizes" menu.

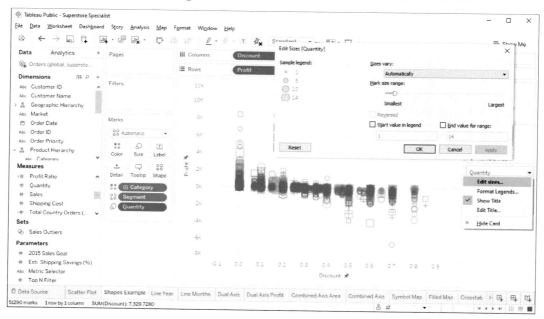

Edit Sizes

The edit sizes menu provides options for how to vary the size and the range of sizes. The menu displays different options for discrete and continuous fields. The size adjustment varies y mark type, and you will need to experiment to find the right combinations and uses.

Remember, just because you can doesn't mean you should add data to the aesthetic layers. While layering information is an excellent tool, it is not always intuitive to read. It may not make sense to the viewer to have the bars on a bar chart different widths, or perhaps, the data doesn't' have enough differentiation to be informative changing the width of lines. Step away for a minute and revisit your visualization if you're unsure, and it is always a good idea to solicit feedback from report users throughout the development press.

Now that we've covered the details on building and formatting individual views, let's take it up a notch with the design and creation of dashboards.

Create and modify a dashboard

Dashboards are a collection of views combined into a single layout. The dashboard layout serves as a guide for running your business. In a business setting, think of your report viewers as a flight crew. They're sitting the cockpit setting the strategic course for the organisation. Much like a pilot they need to navigate economic "airspace," and this requires the right navigational tools.

Navigation is a difficult skill, especially while flying a plane. As a passenger, I want the pilot, and flight crew, to have a working dashboard with all the key indicators they need to fly the plane. When we work for a company, we want the people driving our business to have the information they need to drive success.

To do that people need quick access to the current status and performance of their business areas. Dashboards provide an intuitive, graphical way to represent business trends and measure outcomes. That said, there is also an artistic element to dashboards. Done well they serve as a clever way to provoke thought and communicate ideas in an intuitive, aesthetically pleasing layout.

We will cover adding a dashboard tab, Tableau's dashboard objects, and basic design principles.

Adding a dashboard

Tableau has incredible flexibility with combining worksheet views and other elements into insightful, interactive dashboards. Done right, dashboards allow the viewer to explore the data, navigate their business, and make quick decisions. Successful dashboards assemble and arrange Tableau elements to efficiently communicate a message, without misleading the viewer.

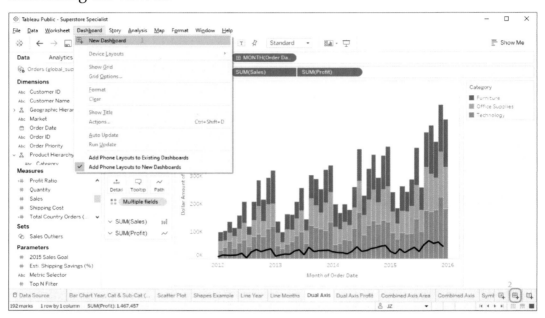

Create Dashboard

There are two ways to add a new dashboard to the workbook.

1. Click the dashboard drop-down in the menu bar, and select "New Dashboard."

2. Or, click the add dashboard button in the workbook tabs.

Dashboard objects and sizing

Successful visual storytelling requires an understanding of the audience, and this understanding includes how they read the dashboard, what device they use, and their area of interest. If everyone in the organization uses the same monitor, you can set the size of the dashboard to fit within a maximized window on the screen.

Tableau has 3 high-level sizing options, fixed, range, and automatic:

- *Fixed* sizing sets static dimensions for the dashboard, and will load faster when there is a cached version on the Tableau server.

- *Range* sizing adjusts the size of the dashboard within a minimum dimensions and maximum dimensions, and is useful when viewers use multiple devices with similar sizes, like mobile phones or tablets.

- *Automatic* sizing makes the dashboard layout fully responsive to the screen and window size, and tends to work best with tiled layouts.

Additionally, Tableau can also store device-specific (Desktop, Tablet, Mobile) layouts and sizes for a dashboard. The sizing menu pops up from the dashboard pane just below the device preview button.

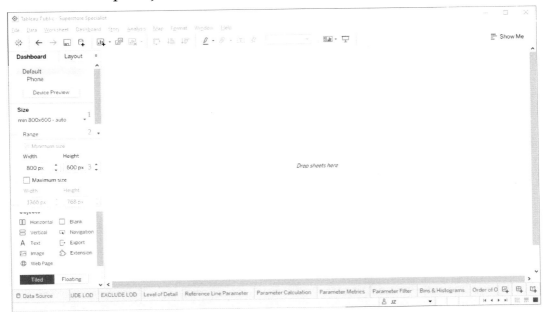

Sizing Controls

1. Click the size drop-down, and the sizing options appear.

2. Select between fixed, range and automatic.

3. Select the resolution from the drop-down menu for fixed sizing, or enter the size(s) manually. *(The fixed sizing drop-down has dimensions that are a useful guide for min and max range sizes.)*

In the image above, the size is set to a minimum of laptop browser (800 x 600), and the maximum size is blank. This means that the dashboard will scale up to fit any screen size greater than 800px x 600px.

Before we start designing and building a dashboard, let's cover some of the features and functionality of the dashboard tab. The image below highlights the dashboard menu item for displaying the dashboard title and the dashboard objects available in Tableau.

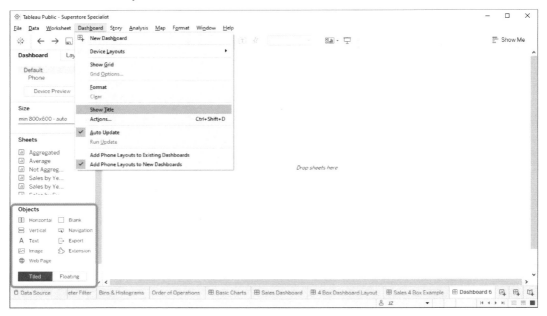

Objects

- **Horizontal** containers allow you to group sheets and other objects side-by-side within the dashboard layout.

- **Vertical** containers allow you to group sheets and other objects one on top of the other within the dashboard layout.

- **Text** objects add custom text and information to the dashboard.

- **Image** objects add image files to the dashboard.

- **Web Page** objects add a space on the dashboard to render a web address as part of the dashboard.

- **Blank** objects empty objects that are useful to force alignment / whitespace within the dashboard.

- **Navigation** objects add a button to the dashboard, and it can be customized to take the viewer to a specific location / view in the workbook. (You can also use custom images for the buttons.)

- **Export** objects add a button to the dashboard, allowing the user to export the dashboard in the specified format.

- **Extension** objects add custom web apps capable of two-way communication with your Tableau dashboard. *(These are well beyond the scope of the Tableau Desktop Specialist exam.)*

Before we move on, let's talk about containers. Containers are the key to maximizing the dynamic capabilities of Tableau. It's easy enough to use filters and parameters to make the data in the charts dynamic and interactive, but the containers make the entire layout dynamic and interactive.

Adding objects to the dashboard

There are two ways to add these objects to the dashboard. The first option is to drag and drop them to your desired location. The second is to double-click the object, and Tableau will automatically place it on the dashboard canvas. The placement of the object will vary based on whether the toggle at the bottom of the objects pane is set to Tiled or Floating.

Tableau places tiled objects on a single layer grid that adjusts the sizing in response to the size of the dashboard. Tableau places floating objects on multiple layers based on the item hierarchy in the layout tab, and you can combine tiled and floating objects. Floating objects tend produce the best results with fixed size and position.

To illustrate some of the functionality thus far, let's add the dual axis chart and the scatter plot onto the dashboard as a tiled objects.

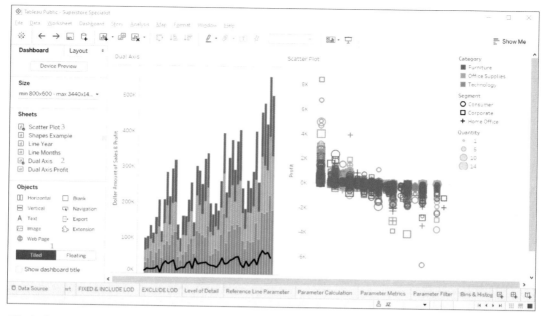

Tiled Object

1. Select the tiled object option

2. Double-click the sheet with the combined axis area chart.

3. Double-click the filled map sheet. (You can also drag the sheet to your desired location.)

Tableau places the legend and any filter controls in a side-bar on the right, and splits the remaining space equally between the two views. The side-bar will remain, and adding additional views, subdivides the view space. Tableau will add each new sheet object in the following order, top left, top right, bottom left, bottom right. The charts resize with each new object to split the view space equally between them.

Notice in the image above that the length of the two charts distorts the views. The lines look much steeper, implying a larger increase than actually present in the data, and the map zoomed out so far that most of the chart space is empty. If we specify the layout settings, we can make sure that the auto-sizing doesn't distort the message.

The layout tab is in the dashboard pane, and it contains controls for size, location, padding, and other layout elements. You can access the layout tab with a mouse-click, or by pressing "T" on your keyboard. The image below shows the layout tab with 4 sheets added to the dashboard using Tableau's default placement, which works pretty well (*more on this in a bit*).

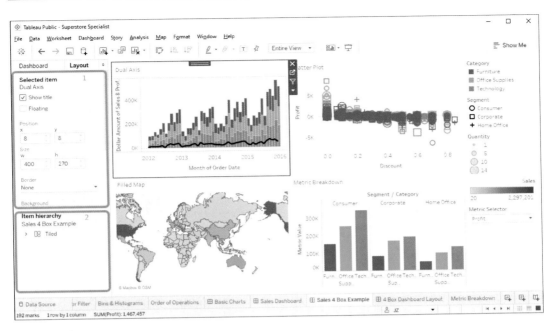

Layout Tab

Depending on the size of your monitor and Tableau window, there may be a scroll bar within the layout tab so you can access all the options. You can use the layout tab to adjust the following settings, in addition to toggle buttons for the selected object's title and float setting.

- **Position** sets the location of the top left corner for floating objects using x and y pixel coordinates.

- **Size** sets the width and height dimensions of the object in pixels.

- **Border** line type, color, and weight for object borders.

- **Background** sets the dashboard background color. (*This will not change the chart background color, that must be done on the chart worksheet.*)

- **Outer Padding** adjusts the buffer (space) between the object edges and other dashboard objects.

- **Inner Padding** adjusts the buffer (space) between the object edges and its internal charts / objects.

- **Item Hierarchy** controls the order of items for floating objects with respect layering on the dashboard, and for tiled objects, it is a useful tool to select objects by name.

These layout options are the key to mastering the final details of your dashboard, and when combined with a strong working knowledge of dashboard containers, there is almost no limit to what you can build in Tableau.

Dashboard design principles

What's the first thing you need to tell the viewer to set the context and trigger a question? The visual containing that information should take the anchor point at the top left. The rest of the layout builds on the initial idea from the first view.

Most viewers read dashboards from from left to right, following the arrows in the image below. That makes the top-left object a key anchor point in most dashboards. It's the first thing the viewer sees, and the anchor point needs capture their interest, pulling the viewer into the visual.

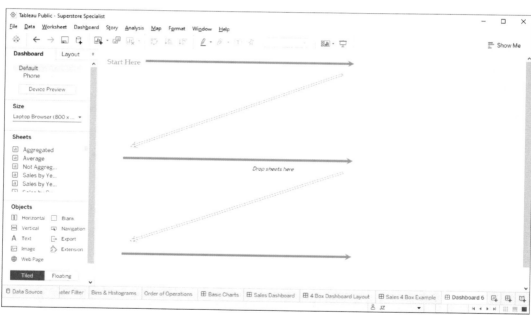

Blank Dashboard

Ideally, that first item prompts the viewer to ask a question, like, "Why are sales so high there, or what about the consumer segment?" The next item should answer the viewer's initial question, while prompting a follow-up question. This should continue as they progress through the dashboard. When they arrive at the end of the dashboard, they should be at a conclusion, or completely hooked so they click through to the next view.

Follow this line of interrogation as you design your dashboard. Start the design by experimenting in Tableau with the different views, but personally, I like to grab a piece of piece of paper to make a rough sketch. I find this approach forces me to be more intentional with the questions I'm asking and answering.

Let's start with a simple 4-box dashboard layout. In the example above, we added two different sheets as tiled objects by double-clicking them. If we continue with two more sheets, then Tableau will produce a 4 box layout with the legends and any filter controls in a vertical bar on the right side of the dashboard.

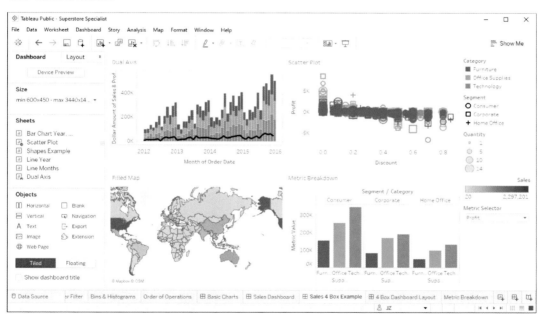

4 Box Default Tableau Placement

Now let's revisit the default Tableau placement. The default 4-box placement is a workable start for a dashboard, but adding more than 4 visuals distorts the size of the charts. Tableau automatically resizes them to fit the space, and this impacts the aspect ratios.

For most chart types, a landscape orientation provides the least distorted view. There is a healthy debate on the exact dimensions, but the width should be 1.5 to 1.8 times the height. The goal is maximization a chart's information value, without distorting the content. The exact ratio changes a bit with the type of chart. Longer time periods, or continuous ranges, may require more width, and depending on the value range and number of dimensions, discrete values on the x-axis may call for a shorter width. Typically, a 45-degree slope provides a good level of detail, and you can fine tune the width and height to achieve the desired slope angle. Notice in the image below, the steeper slope over-accentuates increases and decreases, whereas the flatter slope hides the movement in values.

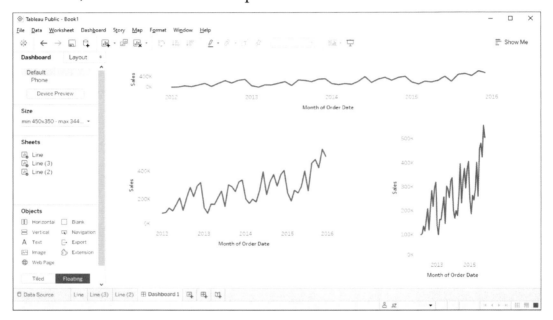

Chart Dimensions

Using a blank dashboard, spend time experimenting with the size of the charts you created. How might the viewer's interpretation of the visual change at different sizes and aspect ratios?

Tweaking the Layout

Now that we have a 4 box layout, let's refine it into a better visual depiction of sales and profit. In the top left quadrant, use the Dual Axis sales and profit chart from section 4. That provides a baseline for revenue and profit, and a likely follow-up question is, 'Why isn't the profit ratio increasing with the revenue. To include that information, we can use the scatter plot of profit versus discount. This let's the viewer investigate whether the discounts are negatively impacting the profitability across category and segment. Next, we can use the choropleth to map the geographic sales, and let the viewer investigate the difference in sales and profit by location. Finally, we can include a details view of the volumes by segment and category.

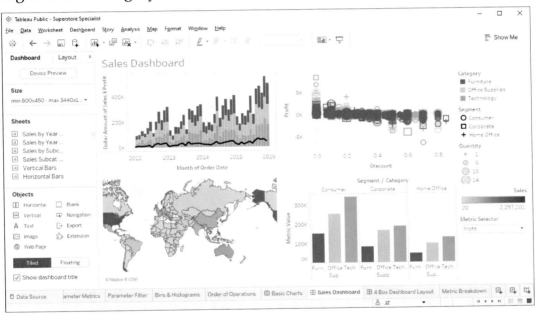

Sales Dashboard

The first enhancement to the default layout, will be color. Since red implies a critical, possibly negative values, we will change technology to orange, and use a lighter blue for office supplies. To ensure, consistent coloring, change the default property for the category dimension back on one of the worksheets. Additionally, let's drop the chart titles, making space for more descriptive axis labels.

Before we add additional interactive elements, enhance your map and scatter plot so they respond to metric selector, and let's move the legend and parameter controls. We will make the metric selector and the map legend floating objects, and relocate them to create space for larger charts.

Floating Objects

1. Click the parameter selector object, and bring up the drop down menu.

2. Click "Floating" to change the object to a floating object.

3. Drag the floating object to the white space above the charts, to the right of the dashboard title.

4. Repeat the process for the map's color legend, placing the floating object at the bottom center of the map. (Pictured in the next image.)

For the remaining legend objects, we will add a floating container to the dashboard, and move the legends from the side bar into the floating object. Then we add a button to show/hide the legends.

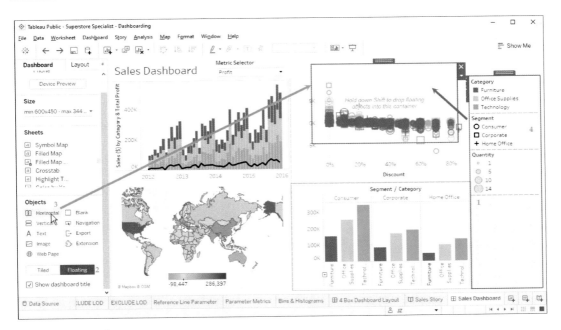

Relocate Legends

1. Select the container on the right with the legends. Notice that it is a vertical container that stacks the legends on top of each other, indicated by the dashed, horizontal lines.

2. Click the floating button,

3. Drag a horizontal container into the dashboard.

4. Finally, drag the legends into the container one at a time, before adjusting the container and legend sizes to fit the white space above the scatter plot. (See the next image)

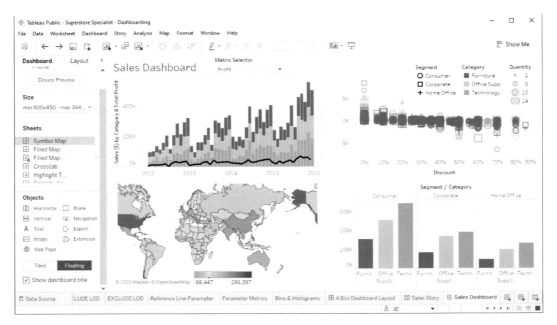

Final Legend Placement

Moving the legends and parameter control use the space on the dashboard more efficiently, but the legends take away from the scatter plot slightly.

Add interactive or explanatory elements

The goal for the dashboard design is to be intuitive, interactive and, most importantly, informative. We already have the parameter selector in the dashboard, but we could add additional filters, using the drop-down menus for the chart objects. There is an option to add the filter controls for any charts with filters.

Layering explanatory and interactive elements achieves these goals. We can add additional explanatory detail to the graphs with the detail in the tool tip, as well as text boxes, but first we will use a button to let viewers hide the legends, once they know what the colors and symbols represent.

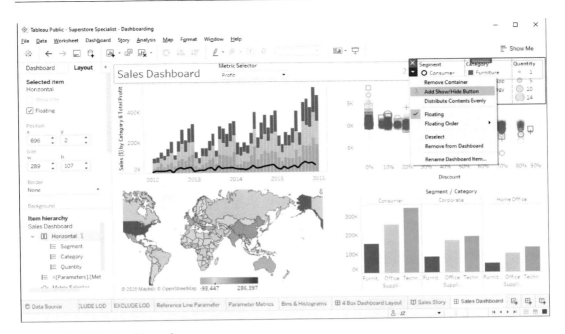

Interactive Sales Dashboard

1. Go to the layout tab and select the horizontal container with the legend objects.

2. Click the dropdown menu for the container object.

3. Click the menu item to "Add Show/Hide Button."

Now there will be a clickable X next to the legends, and when pressed, the button collapses the legends into a hamburger menu!

Next up, lets add a text object next to the parameter control to serve as an explanatory element, guiding the viewer through the dashboard controls.

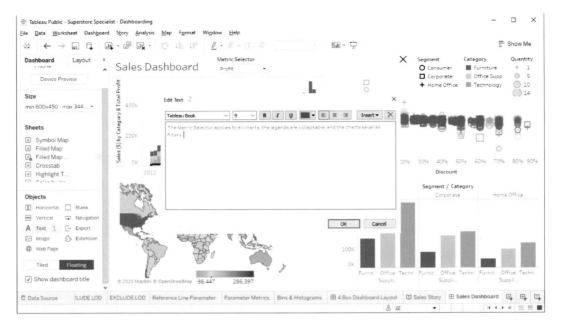

Explanatory Element

1. With the floating objects selected, double-click the text object to add a textbox to the dashboard.

2. Add a brief explanation for how the controls work, and edit the size and font.

3. Resize the text box, and drag it into place between the metric selector and the legends.

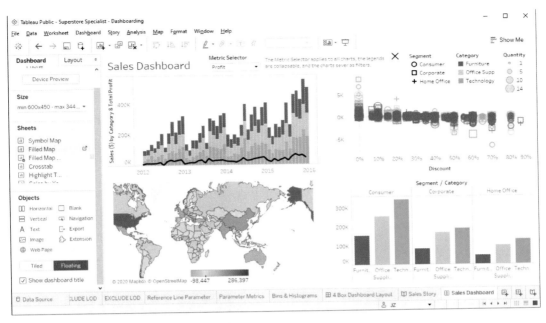

Interactive Dashboard w/ Explanatory Element

With the description, it is clear to the viewer how the report functions. Little cues for the dashboard viewer go a long way. As you finalize the design, make time to improve the tooltips for the charts included on the dashboard. Tooltips bring up relevant details when the viewer hovers their mouse cursor over a specific mark on the visualizations, and well thought out tooltips allow the viewer to probe deeper, without requiring additional charts and tables.

Let's add some dashboard actions, and then we can create a mobile layout, before the final stretch our Tableau Desktop Specialist journey.

Add dashboard actions

Adding actions to the dashboard extends its interactive capability. We can use actions to enhance the dynamic visuals and interactions within Tableau, and we can also use actions to extend the viewer experience beyond Tableau. Here is a list of available actions.

- Filter - filter actions apply a filter to specified visualizations when a viewer interacts with a chart designated for use as a filter.

- Highlight - highlight actions will highlight dimensions similar to the highlighting when selecting a legend item.

- Go to URL - this navigates the user to a web page, either in a new browser window / tab or within a web page object on the dashboard.

- Go to Sheet - this navigates the user to a dashboard, sheet or story within a workbook.

- Change Parameter - this allows parameter controls to be set using values from the visualization.

- Change Set Values - set actions allow the viewer to add and remove values from a set by interacting with dashboard visualizations.

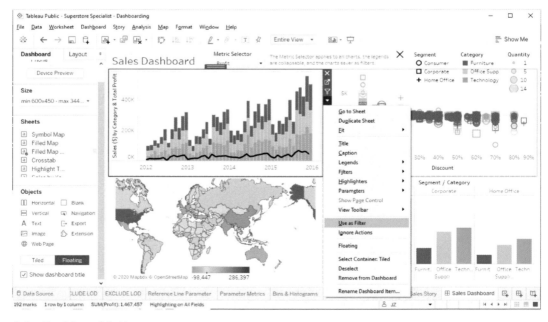

Sales Dashboard Action

First, let's add a filter action, which is probably the easiest. Simply, select a chart, and click "Use as Filter" in the drop-down menu.

The use as filter setting creates a default dashboard action to filter the other visuals based on the selected mark. This setting is available on all of charts, and is a great way to save the space filter controls occupy. Holding the "Control" (Windows) or "Command" (Mac) buttons while clicking selects multiple marks to expand the filter options. Using the sales and profit time series let's the viewer select a cross section of month, and category to filter the entire dashboard.

After we've added the "Use as filter" action to the remaining charts, we can explore the "Actions" controls from the Dashboard drop-down in the menubar.

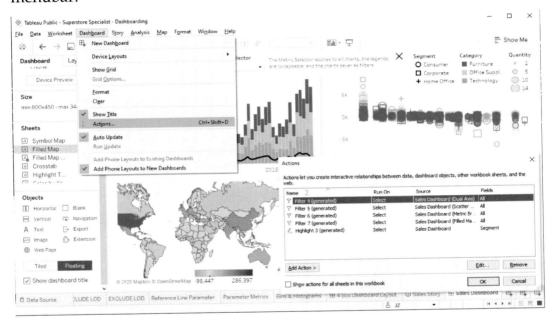

Actions Menu

1. Select "Actions."

2. Select an action in the actions dialogue box, and click "Edit"

This brings up the edit actions box, which also includes an option for creating custom actions from scratch. Adding or editing an action brings up a dialogue box with the various options for the action. The image below contains the settings for one of the filter actions.

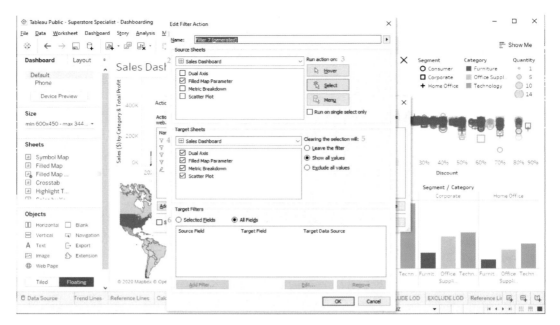

Actions Dialogue Box

1. Name: Filter 7(Generated) is not particularly descriptive. When there are multiple actions, be as descriptive as possible with the names.

2. Source Sheets: The source sheet drives the action, and the available options depend on the dashboard selection.

3. Run action on: This determines whether the action runs when the view hovers of the sheet, selects marks within a sheet, or right-clicks to access the drop-down menu.

4. Target Sheers: This determines where Tableau applies the action. For the filter action these are the sheets where Tableau applies the filter.

5. Clearing the selection: This specifies whether Tableau should leave the filter in place, remove the filter to show all values, or exclude all values, when the use moves the mouse, clears the selection, or changes the menu.

6. Target Filters: Determines the fields used for filtering, or highlighting.

The options in the actions editor change slightly, depending on the action type, but overall, the edit action box contains settings for Tableau's target response to a viewer's interaction with a specified source.

There are endless ways to use these actions, and the with each new update possibilities continue to grow. As an example, it is possible to use floating containers to show and hide different visuals using filter actions, and you can use the URL actions to integrate seamlessly with web resources. The detail for these actions is beyond the scope of the Specialist exam. However, the online Tableau community is constantly sharing inventive uses of actions, and I highly recommend getting involved there to develop your Tableau expertise.

Modify existing dashboard layout for mobile devices

Once the interactive dashboard is ready to go for the desktop, it's important to consider the users who may access charts on mobile or tablet devices. Mobile became so popular that Tableau now adds a default mobile layout to every dashboard. However, it is important to preview the phone layout, and if there are lots of tablet users, you should generate an additional tablet layout. To edit the default phone layout, click the lock icon in the dashboard pane.

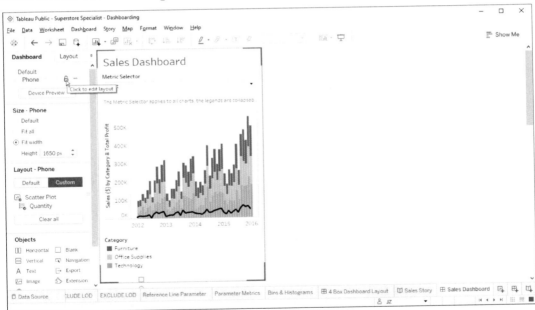

Default Phone Layout

Some pre-existing dashboards may not have a default phone layout, and in these cases you will need to add one. These are the same steps for adding a tablet layout, as well.

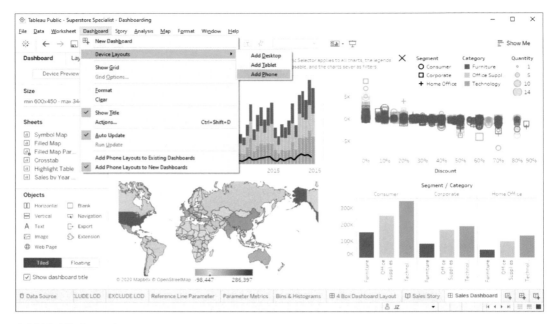

Add Mobile Layout

Working with the mobile layout is identical to our earlier dashboard creation prices, with a few exceptions.

Given the smaller canvas size, and the user interface, there are additional considerations with respect to the layout. In case the viewer is using mobile data, phone layouts require optimisation for quicker rendering, and the layout needs tweaks, so the viewer has enough white space to scroll without accidentally selecting a mark or legend entry.

If your organization issues the same phone to staff, then you can use the specific dimensions of that device. You can also use the device preview to create layouts for multiple devices.

Before reading on, examine the image below for any adjustments you think it requires.

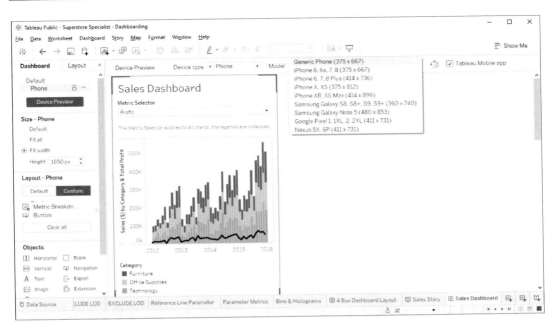

Mobile Device Layout

Notice the device preview menu includes options for device type (Desktop, Tablet, Mobile), and for each type there is a list of specific devices / layout dimensions. There are also two toggles on the far right, one for portrait vs. landscape orientation, and the other for the Tableau Mobile App.

Viewing the dashboard through the app is most common, due to security requirements, but it is important to consider whether users will be in their phone browser or the app.

In addition to the device dimensions, the number of mobile tweaks required depends on the original layout and complexity of the dashboard. With our sales dashboard, Tableau inserts our floating objects as tiled, and some of the text is truncated. Let's walk through the adjustments we need to make and some important considerations for viewer experience.

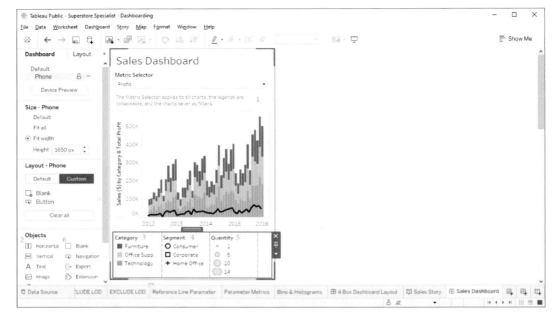

Mobile Layout Adjustments

1. Use the text object's drop-down menu to edit the height, and set it to 42. This way the full text displays.

2. Add a horizontal container in between the "Category" legend and the profit graph.

3. Drag the "Category" legend into the horizontal container.

4. Drag the "Segment" legend into the horizontal container.

5. Drag the "Quantity" legend into the horizontal container.

6. Add a blank object to the far right of the horizontal container so there is whitespace for the viewer to scroll.

Now we have a solid opening view. While two of the legends don't pertain to the visible chart, their marks make that fairly obvious, and they do apply to the first chart the viewer sees when scrolling down. What adjustments need to happen as the viewer continues to scroll?

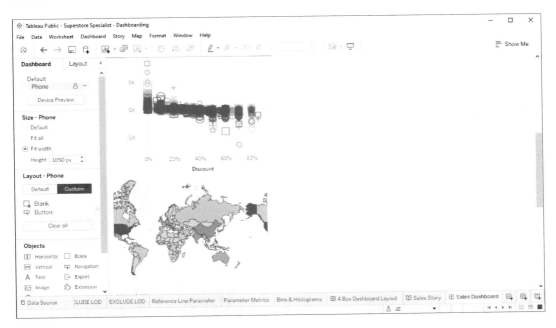

Continuing to scroll

As the viewer continues to scroll down, they run out of white space to use for scrolling, and it is not immediately clear what the scale is for the map.

To improve the layout, we can use another horizontal container between the scatterplot and the map. Inside the container we can add the map legend, along with two blank objects on either side. This helps the viewer interpret the map as soon as they see it, and it also provides whitespace for the user to scroll.

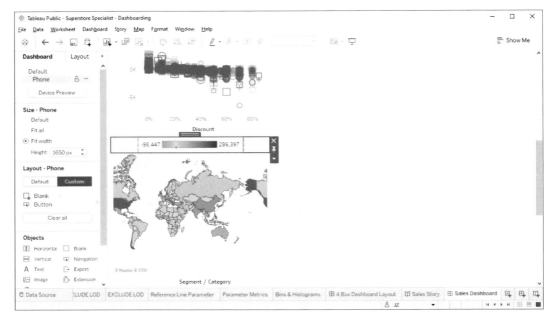

Map Legend Adjustment

Now there is one final consideration regarding the fourth graph. Notice the labels on the horizontal axis in the image below.

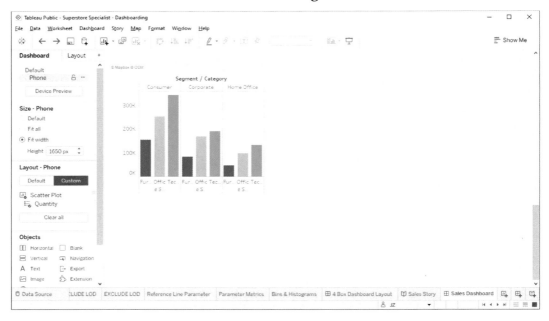

Category Axis Labels

The horizontal labels on the x-axis provide a better aspect ratio for the chart on the desktop layout, but here Tableau truncates most of the label text. The best fix for some of these formatting options is to create a duplicate sheet, specifically for the mobile layout. Then, we can set different label orientation for mobile and desktop. However, the labels may not add enough information value to justify maintaining multiple copies of the worksheet.

In this instance it is a style decision. The segment / category view is the fourth chart, and it uses the same color scheme from the first two charts. Therefore, the labels are somewhat arbitrary.

Having addressed these key considerations, we now have a dashboard that is ready to publish for both the desktop and mobile users.

In our example, we used a range to size our dashboard to fit on smaller laptop screens and large desktop monitors. This will likely work well with modern tablets. However, if there are display issues for tablet users, add a tablet device layout following the same steps from the phone layout above.

Tableau selects the device layout based on the size of the browser or screen in pixels.

- Phone - 500 pixels or less for phone

- Tablet - 501 to 800 pixels

- Desktop - Greater than 800 pixels

In a corporate setting, there are a range of devices that viewers will use, and there is a growing prevalence of 'bring your own device' programs. This means having multiple device layouts is increasingly more important.

For a deeper dive into some of the advanced dashboard and layout features, check out the Tableau site[34].

Create a story using dashboards or views

Stories are a sequential combination of worksheets and dashboards, and they serve as a guided tour through the insights contained in a workbook. At its essence, a story is another sheet in the workbook so many of the same techniques and methods from dashboards and sheets apply to naming an layout. For the specialist exam, you will only need to be able to answer a high-level question or two, because there is no way to grade a story with multiple choice questions.

There are two ways to add a story to your workbook.

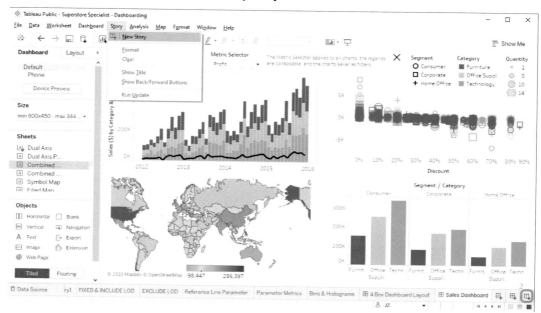

Add Story Menu

1. Click the "Story" dropdown menu on the story bar and select "New Story."

2. Click the story icon in the layout buttons.

This brings up a blank story workspace, and most of the options should be intuitive at this point. On the left side of the window is the story pane, which includes a layout tab. The only options for the story layout tab are the button styles to navigate through the story points. Each slide, or navigation stop, in a Tableau story is referred to as a story point. The default story point layout is caption boxes, but there are 3 additional options. My recommendation is either to use the dots or the captions. Captions help to frame the story, while the dots take up the least space. With dots, you'll have more room for the visuals. For our example we will use the captions.

Story Workspace

1. Choose whether or not to display the story title.

2. The first adjustment to make is size because this sets the canvas for adding the visuals. Here, it is set to the same range from the dashboard example, 600 x 450px to 3440 x 1440px.

3. Add captions for points you want to make. (Start by outlining your points, and then come back through and select the visuals that tell the story.)

4. Now it is time to add visualizations and text notes to the story points.

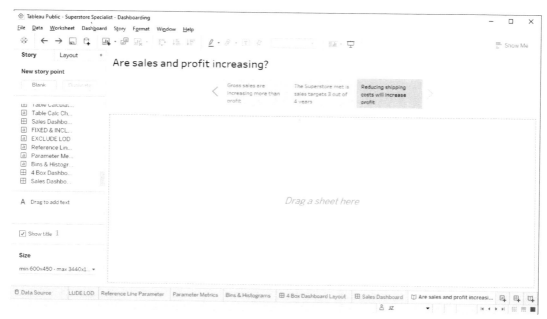

Titled and Outlined

Stories tend to answer questions, and the questions make for good titles. Here, we'll tell the story of the increasing sales, and whether or not there is a corresponding increase in profitability, considering costs and other factors. Let' add visuals and commentary to back up our story points.

Add to Story

Tableau displays a thumbnail when you hover the mouse over an item in the list of worksheets in dashboards, and when you find the visual you want to add, there are two ways to add it to the story point. It is the same functionality as the worksheets and dashboards, either drag or double-click.

Once we have the story point visual, we can drag in text to include additional commentary beyond the short caption in the navigation controls. As an example, I added some notes about the sales trajectory and what might be impacting profitability.

Short story example

Now we add the visuals to the story points on sales targets and shipping costs. I've selected the reference and trend lines chart with a few tweaks, and the combined axis chart with profit and shipping represented by an area chart. In working through the text for the slides, Sometimes, during the process, you may decide to rearrange, add, and remove story points. New story points appear at the end of the sequence, but simply click and drag them to the desired order.

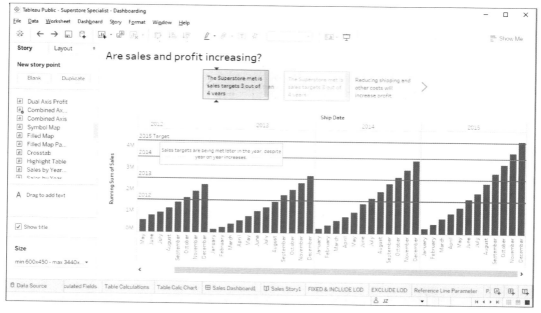

Arranging Story Points

This concludes what you need to know about stories for the Specialist exam. However, most of this can be done more effectively using dashboards, navigation buttons and parameter actions. The story interface is quite limited, and probably one of the least used features of Tableau.

For more on stories, check the Tableau site[35].

Share a twbx as an image

It's quite easy to share visualizations from a Tableau workbook as images and PDFs. These features are limited to Tableau Desktop, and if you're preparing for the exam with Tableau Public, you can practice with the 14-day free trial. I recommend the free-trial for final preparation, when you book the exam. That said you need to remember three things:

1. You print to PDF.

2. You export images and PowerPoint files.

3. You downloaded images from a visualization published to a Tableau server.

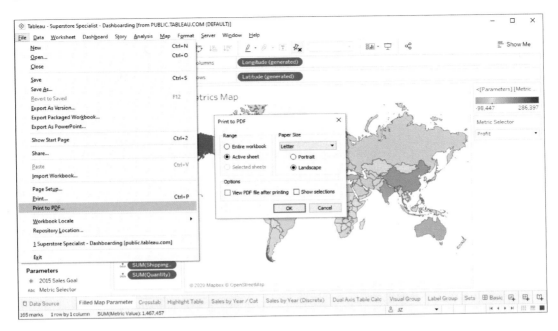

Print PDF

Printing to a PDF follows a standard printing flow. Click the menubar, select "Print to PDF", and set your desired in the dialogue box. Once you specify the desired options, click "OK," and follow the prompts to specify the file name and location.

Alternatively, you can export an image file from Tableau. First we'll review exporting a dashboard as an image file.

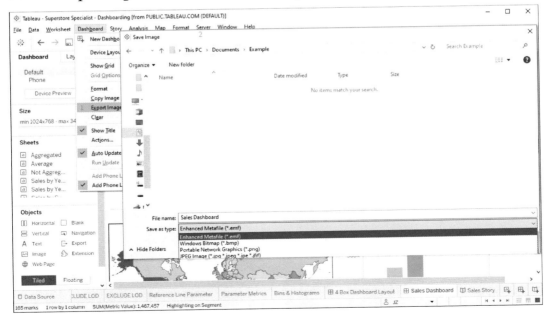

1. Select the "Export Image" option from the Dashboard drop-down in the menubar.

2. Specify the location, filename, and image format, before clicking "Save."

The process is similar for the worksheet. However, the options are slightly different. You select whether or not to include the title, view, caption or legends, as well as the legend placement.

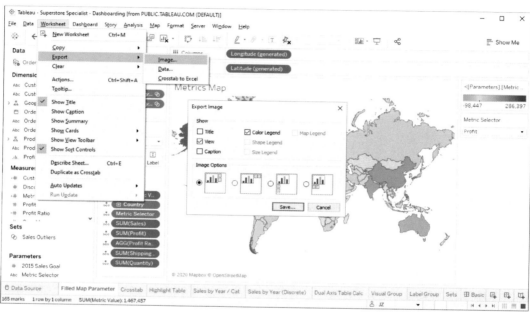

Export Worksheet Image

The final visual export option is PowerPoint. Selecting "File" in the menubar, click the option for "Export as PowerPoint," and specify the sheets to include as slides, before following the save file prompts for location and filename.

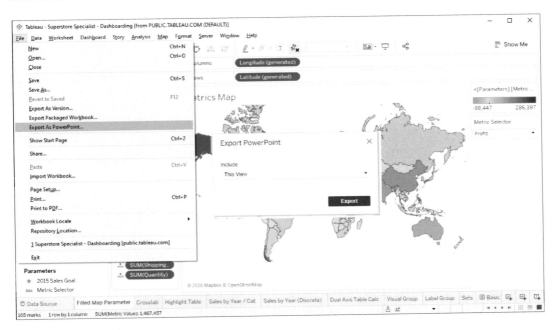

Export to PowerPoint

Timeliness & Conclusion

Timeliness

"Completing a task effectively and efficiently has become a standard that organizations expect from employees. This exam is timed because we view time as a critical competency needed to be successful."

That is a direct quote from the Tableau Desktop Specialist Exam Prep Guide[36], and it highlights the challenge presented in the real world.

Sometimes, you will have the ability to invest months into the perfect visualizations, but most of the time you will need to produce a functional visualization that drives insights and actions, as quickly as possible. This means publish something, soliciting feedback, and then iterating through that process until it's time to move on to the next project.

Challenge yourself to make a new dashboard every day, and before long, you'll have some go to recipes and layouts to answer the common questions you receive, within the desired time frames of your customers.

In this spirit, the Tableau Desktop Specialist is a timed exam. Go through the exam and answer all the questions where you immediately know the answer. Then go back through the remaining questions to work through the answers. This way you get points for everything you know, and you'll know just how much time you have to work through the harder questions.

Conclusion

This book endeavors to prepare you for the Tableau Desktop specialist exam, with enough real-world context to help you build the portfolio you need to land your next data gig. That said, this book barely scratches the surface of Tableau's capabilities.

With Tableau, you can create stunning infographics for print publications, and you can construct dynamic dashboard layouts that reshape based on viewer interaction and dynamically swap chart, and you can even create functioning games and musical instruments!

Now, go schedule your exam for a couple weeks out, and keep practicing. Congratulations on getting this far and good luck with the exam!!!

Acknowledgements

This book was a massive effort, and I want to thank everyone who provided feedback and encouragement along the way.

Notably, my wife Erin, who helped with editing, gentle ribbing, and encouragement. She also subjected herself to a run through of the book with out any prior Tableau knowledge or input from me to confirm it actually works.

Thank you, Frances Jones, for help with edits and structural notes on one of the earliest versions.

Next up, my mate Nic Rivers, who kept checking-in on the progress. This accountability helped me maintain progress, even if it was glacial progression of fits and starts.

Thanks to Jak Krumholtz for the fabulous cover design.

I also need to thank Mom and Dad for raising me with an "anything is possible" mindset.

Another early inspiration was Vincent Pugliese and his freedom crew. Thanks for motivating me to keep searching until I found something that would stick.

Finally, the biggest thanks go to Kouadio Dongo and the Big Data Analytics Partners crew. Kouadio had an idea I should teach some classes and preparing for those classes led to the book. All the amazing individuals who took part in the evolution of those classes provided valuable input in the design and material for the book. Thank you Abiyou, Alex, Bernard, Amandine, Yeo, Blaise, Samuel, Celine, Eugene, Karl, Marcel, Arnauld, Emma, Yaro, Franck, Hermann, Marie Claire, Jean Pacome, and Virginie!

Links & Endnotes

1 https://www.tableau.com/learn/certification/desktop-specialist

2 https://www.tableaudesktopspecialist.com

3 https://public.tableau.com/profile/john.zugelder

4 https://public.tableau.com/

5 https://help.tableau.com/current/pro/desktop/en-us/environment_workspace.htm

6 https://vita.had.co.nz/papers/tidy-data.html

7 https://help.tableau.com/current/pro/desktop/en-us/exampleconnections_overview.htm

8 https://help.tableau.com/current/pro/desktop/en-us/joining_tables.htm

9 https://www.tableau.com/learn/tutorials/on-demand/join-types-union?product=tableau_desktop%2Btableau_prep&version=tableau_desktop_2019_2%2Btableau_prep_2019_2_1&topic=connecting_data

10 https://help.tableau.com/current/pro/desktop/en-us/union.htm

11 https://www.tableau.com/learn/tutorials/on-demand/data-blending?product=tableau_desktop&version=tableau_desktop_2019_2&topic=connecting_data

12 https://help.tableau.com/current/pro/desktop/en-us/multiple_connections.htm

13 https://help.tableau.com/current/pro/desktop/en-us/maps_build.htm

14 https://www.tableau.com/solutions/maps

15 https://help.tableau.com/current/pro/desktop/en-us/buildexamples_maps.htm

16 The estimate is from published articles citing Intelligent Data Corporation, and the assumption is that Mars will be at its closest orbital position to earth. :)

17 https://help.tableau.com/current/pro/desktop/en-us/sortgroup_groups_creating.htm

18 https://help.tableau.com/current/pro/desktop/en-us/sortgroup_sets_create.htm

19 https://help.tableau.com/current/pro/desktop/en-us/tips_visualcues.htm

20 https://help.tableau.com/current/pro/desktop/en-us/sortgroup_sorting_computed_howto.htm

21 https://help.tableau.com/current/pro/desktop/en-us/reference_lines.htm#Add_a_Reference_Line

[22] https://help.tableau.com/current/pro/desktop/en-us/trendlines_add.htm#modeltype

[23] https://help.tableau.com/current/pro/desktop/en-us/environ_workspace_analytics_pane.htm#custom-reference-line

[24] https://help.tableau.com/current/pro/desktop/en-us/calculations_calculatedfields.htm

[25] https://help.tableau.com/current/pro/desktop/en-us/calculations_tablecalculations.htm

[26] https://help.tableau.com/current/pro/desktop/en-us/functions_functions_tablecalculation.htm

[27] https://public.tableau.com/profile/john.zugelder#!/

[28] https://help.tableau.com/current/pro/desktop/en-us/calculations_calculatedfields_lod_overview.htm

[29] https://www.tableau.com/learn/whitepapers/understanding-lod-expressions

[30] https://www.tableau.com/about/blog/LOD-expressions

[31] https://help.tableau.com/current/pro/desktop/en-us/order_of_operations.htm

[32] https://community.tableau.com/ideas/6906

[33] https://help.tableau.com/current/pro/desktop/en-us/formatting_create_custom_colors.htm

[34] https://help.tableau.com/current/pro/desktop/en-us/dashboards.htm
[35] https://help.tableau.com/current/pro/desktop/en-us/stories.htm

[36] https://www.tableau.com/learn/certification/desktop-specialist

Made in United States
Orlando, FL
14 January 2022

13486737R00142